DHAL

NITISHA PATEL

DHAL

COMFORTING VEGAN & VEGETARIAN RECIPES MADE WITH LENTILS, PEAS & BEANS

Photography by Clare Winfield

RYLAND PETERS & SMALL

Senior Designer Sonya Nathoo
Commissioning Editor Alice Sambrook
Creative Director Leslie Harrington
Editorial Director Julia Charles
Production Controller Gordana Simakovic

Food Stylist Maud Eden
Prop Stylist Tony Hutchinson
Indexer Hilary Bird

Originally published as *The Delicious Book of Dhal* in 2019. This updated edition published in 2026 by
Ryland Peters & Small
20–21 Jockey's Fields
London WC1R 4BW
and
1452 Davis Bugg Road
Warrenton, NC 27589

www.rylandpeters.com
email: euregulations@rylandpeters.com

10 9 8 7 6 5 4 3 2 1

ISBN 978-1-78879-744-3

Printed in China

A CIP record for this book is available from the British Library. US Library of Congress cataloging-in-Publication Data has been applied for.

The authorised representative in the EEA is Authorised Rep Compliance Ltd., Ground Floor, 71 Lower Baggot Street, Dublin, D02 P593, Ireland
www.arccompliance.com

MIX
Paper | Supporting responsible forestry
FSC® C106563

NOTES

- Both British (Metric) and American (Imperial plus US cups) measurements are included in these recipes for your convenience. However it is important to work with one set of measurements and not alternate between the two within a recipe.
- All spoon measurements are level unless otherwise specified.
- Ovens should be preheated to the specified temperatures. We recommend using an oven thermometer. If using a fan-assisted oven, adjust temperatures according to the manufacturer's instructions.
- When a recipe calls for the grated zest of citrus fruit, buy unwaxed fruit and wash well before using. If you can only find treated fruit, scrub well in warm soapy water before using.

CONTENTS

INTRODUCTION

'Okay, the dhal baath is ready,' Mum would call out to the house most Saturday afternoons. 'Yum! Do we have lime pickle too?,' would quickly come my eager reply.

Growing up in an Indian family, this is one of the fondest food memories from my childhood. If we didn't have somewhere to be and were spending Saturday at home, without fail, my mum would be busy making a big pot of 'dhal baath' (curried lentils and rice).

As an adult, eating dhal still arouses these treasured memories for me. Most comfort food from childhood is evocative, but in my opinion, dhals in particular have the ability to transport you to another world, with their aromatic spices and warming, nourishing taste. When I began to cook dhal myself, this added another layer of satisfaction – with the realization that even the simplest of cooking processes can create this soul-stroking bowl of wholesome goodness.

Dhal is the term used all over India for dried split lentils, beans and peas. It refers to both the ingredient as well as the final cooked dish. From a young age, I was always fascinated with the many varieties of dried dhal. I was drawn to the jars-upon-jars of multi-coloured 'pearls' that lined my mum's store cupboard shelves – from tiny orange specks to black beads, shiny maroon gems, to yellow discs and emerald green orbs – such a vast array of shapes and colours!

What I love most about dhal is not only the range of various types, each with their own characteristic flavour and texture, but the endless variety of recipes that can be created with it. From stews to soups, curries to pancakes, fritters to desserts, the list of lentil-based dishes is extensive to say the least.

And lentil-based recipes have never been as widely relevant outside India as they are now. Especially as a food consultant, it's evident to me that we as a generation are more health conscious and environmentally aware than ever before, and this is directly impacting what we eat. Vegan and vegetarian diets are becoming ever more common, as we realize that rearing vast quantities of animals for food also puts strain on our land and agricultural resources.

Substituting a meat-based meal with a vegan or vegetarian meal at least once or twice a week has great benefits for our health and the environment, yet to some people still, this change can seem daunting (especially when, to some, a vegan diet means just salad!). But hopefully, this book is proof that dhal is a dish that won't leave you wanting. Here, I share some of my favourite recipes for the most traditionally popular types of dhal, along with some unique modern recipes. They include a rainbow of vegetables and an array of herbs, spices, toppings and accompaniments, so that whenever you need something wholesome yet comforting, you will always find that you can turn to a delicious bowl of dhal.

COOKING DHAL AND GETTING IT RIGHT

There are so many types of dhal and some crossover in the terminology, which can lead to confusion. In order to confidently cook with dhal and get it right, it is important to understand the distinctions.

In the UK, dried lentils, beans or peas (whether whole or split) all come under the umbrella term 'pulse'. In the UK and US, lentils, beans and peas are all classified as legumes, whether fresh, dried, whole or split – so pulses are part of the legume family.

Lentils are usually disc shaped, with a slightly thicker middle. In the West and across Europe, firm-cooked brown or green lentils are the most commonly eaten. However, in Indian cuisine, masoor dhal (split red lentils) and urad lentils (black with the skin and white without) are more popular, and these are usually cooked until soft.

Split peas used for Indian dhal tend to cook more quickly than whole lentils. The main split peas are channa (split chickpeas), toor (split pigeon peas) and split yellow peas.

Beans used for dhal are generally bigger than lentils or peas. The most common are rajma (red kidney beans) and chori (aduki beans). Left whole and dried, these always require soaking before cooking.

As dhal is so massively integral to Indian cuisine, most Indian kitchens are equipped with a pressure cooker, which helps to shorten the cooking times. However, I've included instructions for cooking all these recipes in a saucepan, too. The more you cook with legumes, the more you will come to understand and perfect the cooking processes involved for each type, but follow this basic guide if you are just starting out.

Toor Dhal (Split Pigeon Peas)

You can cook toor dhal from raw (without soaking) if using a pressure cooker, with a ratio of 1 part toor to 3 parts boiling water for approximately 15 minutes (or 9 whistles). Cook until the lentils are completely softened before adding to the base of your dish. If you don't have a pressure cooker, the toor will need soaking first for 4–5 hours. You can then cook it in a saucepan for 60–70 minutes.

Masoor Dhal (Split Red Lentils)

Probably the quickest and easiest choice if you don't have a pressure cooker, once picked for stones and rinsed, these lentils can be added straight to the base of your dish and simmered until cooked and softened. Because of this, they soak up the flavours of the other ingredients beautifully.

Channa Dhal (Brown Split Chickpeas)
Channa dhal are quite versatile. They can be soaked overnight and then added straight to the base of a simmering dish, before being simmered until softened but still holding their shape. For a soup or stew however, the channa should be cooked in a pressure cooker or for longer in a saucepan, until softened and no longer holding their shape, with more or less water added, depending on the viscosity you are looking for in the sauce.

Urad Dhal (Black Gram)
Due to its black, seed-like appearance, urad dhal must always be very carefully picked before cooking as stones and dirt can be easily camouflaged amongst the lentils. When left whole with the skin on, urad dhal needs soaking for a minimum of 4 hours before cooking. They should then either be boiled or pressure cooked until they are so soft that they are falling apart. Boiling the lentils can take up to 1 hour, or they can be cooked under pressure for approximately 20 minutes.

Moong Dhal (Whole Green or Yellow Split Moong Beans)
For the more common yellow split variety, moong dhal must first be soaked for 2–3 hours. Once soaked, the dhal should be softened enough to be added and finished off in a sauce base. However, some recipes require the dhal to be so soft that it is falling apart to form the body of a soup or curry. In this case, it should be boiled or pressure cooked further. The whole green variety of moong dhal generally takes even longer to cook until tender and should be soaked overnight, then pressure cooked or boiled before being adding to your dish.

Rajma Dhal (Red Kidney Beans)
These beans should always be soaked overnight in boiling water before cooking (1 part beans to 5 parts boiling water). Once soaked, the red kidney beans then need to be cooked in fresh boiling water until soft but still retaining their shape. Be aware that raw red kidney beans contain a harmful chemical, which is killed off when they are cooked through properly at a high temperature. I have provided instructions for cooking the rajma dhal in a saucepan, but I personally find a pressure cooker is more efficient.

Lal Chori Dhal (Red Aduki Beans)
Having been soaked overnight, chori dhal should then be simmered or pressure cooked until they are soft but still holding their shape. Because of their delicate size and beautiful red colour, chori is rarely cooked until falling apart for soups and stews. The exception to this is when it is being used as a paste for a dip or filling.

SPICES FOR YOUR STORE CUPBOARD

Lentils, beans and peas are great at absorbing flavour, and in order to make your dhals sing, you will need a wide range of spices to hand. Rumour has it that Indian food is spicy, and yes, this can be true – but it can also be quite the opposite! Basically, it can be as hot or as mild as you want it to be. Spice levels can vary from dish to dish, from region to region and from occasion to occasion. The key is getting to know your spices and therefore getting the balance right for you. Out of the hundreds of spices there are in Indian cuisine, each one plays a different role and adds a unique element to your dish – there is so much more besides just fierce chilli/chile heat.

It helps me to categorize my spices into whole dried spices, dried spice seeds, dried leaf spices and ground spices. Below is a list of the spices used in the dhal recipes and the properties they contribute to the dish.

WHOLE DRIED SPICES

Cinnamon Stick Aromatic, pungent in taste and slightly sweet.

Cassia Bark pungent in taste, similar odour to cinnamon but with more liquorice notes.

Cloves Highly aromatic in taste, warm and spicy, contain volatile oils.

Cardamom Pods A strong, unique taste with an intensely aromatic, resinous fragrance.

Star Anise Resembles anise in flavour, sightly sweet and spicy.

Dried Kashmiri Chillies/Chiles Add a deep red colour, moderate spice level.

Asafoetida powder Harmonizes and supercharges other flavours, very strong odour.

Black Peppercorns World's most traded spice, spicy heat, citrusy, woody and floral notes.

DRIED SEEDS

Fennel Seeds Liquorice-flavoured, sweet, aromatic, a light and delicate flavour.

Black Mustard Seeds Spicy, aromatic, rustic taste and smoky fragrance.

Cumin Seeds Distinctive earthy aroma, warmly bitter flavours, draws out other natural flavours.

Black Onion Seeds Aromatic onion flavour, fragrant tinge.

Fenugreek Seeds Bitter and slightly astringent, great for creating a smoky depth of flavour.

Coriander Seeds Earthy, nutty flavour with citrus notes.

Ajwain Seeds Pungent version of thyme with a sharp flavour.

LEAF SPICES

Bay Leaves Distinctive flavour and fragrance, a pungent, sharp and bitter taste. Extremely herbal and floral.

Curry Leaves Aromatic leaves, release a deliciously nutty aroma when fried in hot oil.

Fenugreek Leaves Smoky and bitter but an addictive taste. Strong in aroma and distinctive in flavour.

GROUND SPICES

Ground Cumin Penetrating flavour, slightly bitter, nutty taste, powerful aroma.

Ground Coriander A fresh and pleasing aroma with a mild citrus flavour.

Ground Turmeric Mildly aromatic and has scents of orange and ginger. Has a pungent, bitter flavour.

Paprika Powder A woody, earthy aroma that adds a mild sweet flavour to dishes.

Kashmiri Chilli/Chili Powder Mild in taste, but still delivers a good amount of heat. Gives a lovely deep red colour.

Ground Cinnamon A powerful spice that is sweet and intensely fragrant with a warm and woody aroma.

Ground Green Cardamom A wonderful fragrant and floral aroma with an enticing warm spicy-sweet flavour.

Ground Fenugreek Highly aromatic, slightly sour fragrant flavour with a bitter taste.

Methi Powder Smoky flavour and a light bitter taste with a slight level of heat.

Garam Masala A warm spice mix used to enhance the flavour in a dish. Fragrant, floral and earthy.

Ground Ginger Used as a seasoning agent to give a mild level of heat and spice.

Mango Powder (Amchoor) A fruity spice powder with a citrus taste and a slightly sour aroma.

CHUTNEYS AND PASTES

COCONUT CHUTNEY

CHUTNEY BASE

freshly grated flesh of 1 coconut
100 g/1⅓ cups unsweetened desiccated/dried shredded coconut
1 tbsp channa dhal, toasted
1 green chilli/chile
1.5-cm/½-inch piece of fresh ginger, peeled
1 tsp salt
300 ml/1¼ cups water

SEASONED OIL

2 tbsp vegetable oil
1 tsp urad dhal
½ tsp mustard seeds
½ tsp cumin seeds
½ tsp Kashmiri chilli/chili powder
10 fresh curry leaves
pinch of asafoetida powder

TO FINISH

freshly squeezed juice of 1 lime

SERVES 6

Put all the ingredients for the chutney base in a tall measuring jug/cup and blitz together using a stick blender. Set aside until required.

For the seasoned oil, put the oil into a saucepan over a medium heat and add the urad dhal and mustard seeds, allowing the mustard seeds to sizzle and crackle in the hot oil for 30 seconds. Add the cumin seeds and allow them to pop. Add the Kashmiri chilli/chili powder, curry leaves and asafoetida powder and toss in the hot oil.

Pour the hot seasoned oil over the coconut chutney base, add the lime juice and stir well. This chutney is best eaten on the day it's made.

HARIYALI CHUTNEY

100 g/3½ oz. freshly chopped coriander/cilantro
35 g/1 oz. freshly chopped mint leaves
2 green chillies/chiles
freshly squeezed juice of 1½ limes
1 tsp fine sea salt
2 heaped tsp desiccated/dried shredded coconut
1.5-cm/½-inch piece of fresh ginger, peeled
1 tbsp natural/plain yogurt
1 tsp caster/granulated sugar
4 tbsp vegetable oil
1 tsp cumin seeds, toasted

SERVES 5

Blitz together all the ingredients, apart from the cumin seeds, in a food processor. Stir in the cumin seeds and serve or cover and refrigerate for up to 3 days.

HOLY TRINITY PASTE

200 g/7 oz. green chillies/chiles
200 g/7 oz. garlic cloves, peeled
200 g/7 oz. fresh ginger, peeled
50 ml/3½ tbsp vegetable oil
1 tbsp fine sea salt

MAKES 625 G/2½ CUPS

Blitz together all the ingredients in a food processor. Stir in the cumin seeds and serve or cover and refrigerate for up to 3 days.

TOOR DHAL

Also known as split pigeon peas, toor dhal is an ancient legume, believed to have been cultivated for food for the last 3500 years. Currently, India is the largest producer of pigeon peas, and they are popular in Indian cuisine as a diverse ingredient and a valuable source of protein in vegetarian diets. In order to become toor dhal, the whole pigeon pea outer shell is removed and then the shiny yellow peas inside are dried and split. Toor dhal has a very subtle nutty flavour, which is more noticeable when cooked and served firm, rather than cooked until soft and falling apart. It breaks down easily when slow-cooked and is ideal for soups, stews and a whole host of other delicious recipes. Toor dhal can also be found 'oiled' in large supermarkets – but there isn't much of a difference between the oiled and non-oiled varieties other than that the oiled has a nice sheen to it.

TADKA DHAL

This popular recipe showcases the toor dhal in its simplest form. The flavour is enhanced with a tadka, a tempered blend of pungent spices, which infuses every spoonful.

TOOR DHAL BASE

200 g/7 oz. toor dhal
750 ml/3¼ cups boiling water
½ tsp fine sea salt, plus extra to taste
½ tsp ground turmeric

TADKA

3 tbsp vegetable oil
1 tsp cumin seeds
4 garlic cloves, sliced
2 green chillies/chiles, slit in half lengthways
10–12 fresh curry leaves
large pinch of asafoetida powder
2 large tomatoes, roughly chopped
pinch of fine sea salt
1 tsp palm sugar/jaggery
freshly squeezed juice of ½ lemon
5–6 fresh coriander/cilantro stems, roughly chopped, plus extra to garnish
basmati rice, to serve

pressure cooker (optional)

SERVES 2-3

Start by making the dhal base. Pick through the toor dhal to remove any stones. Place it in a colander and rinse under cold running water until the water runs clear. Transfer the rinsed lentils to a pressure cooker with the boiling water, salt and turmeric. Close the pressure cooker and place over a medium heat. Cook for about 15 minutes or 9 whistles. (If you don't have a pressure cooker, you will first need to soak the picked and rinsed lentils in 1 litre/quart of boiling water for 4–5 hours. Drain, then transfer the lentils to a large saucepan with 1 litre/quart of fresh boiling water, the salt and turmeric. Cover with a lid and bring to the boil, then simmer over a medium heat for 60–70 minutes, topping up the boiling water as needed.)

Towards the end of the lentil cooking time, prepare the tadka. Put the vegetable oil into a saucepan over a medium heat. Add the cumin seeds and let them sizzle for 1 minute. Add the garlic slices and fry for 30 seconds until golden brown. Add the chillies/chiles and curry leaves. Gently shake the pan to coat the ingredients in the seasoned oil. Fry for 30 seconds, then add the asafoetida powder. Stir in the tomatoes and salt. Reduce the heat to low and let the tomatoes melt into the tadka oil for 5–6 minutes, stirring regularly.

Meanwhile, when the lentils are softened but still holding their shape, release the steam from the pressure cooker slowly (or remove the pan from the heat). Most of the cooking water should have been absorbed, but gently crush the lentils with any that remains.

Add the cooked lentils, palm sugar/jaggery and lemon juice to the tomato mixture and mix well. Simmer gently for a final 6–7 minutes.

To finish, mix in the chopped coriander/cilantro and season to taste with salt again before serving. Garnish the dhal with extra coriander/cilantro, if you like, and serve with basmati rice.

DAHI TADKA DHAL AND SPICED MATOKI

This recipe elevates the humble tadka dhal to a rich centrepiece of a main course. The lentil base is lifted with an aromatic tadka of whole spices, fried tomatoes, ginger and garlic, and is finished off with creamy yogurt. The end result is beautifully balanced in flavour. Rather than pairing this North Indian dhal with bread or rice, this recipe pays homage to my Indian and African heritage and instead pairs with spicy South African-style matoki chips. These are shallow-fried plantain slices, dusted with a mix of Himalayan sea salt, black pepper and amchoor (dried mango powder).

TOOR DHAL BASE

200 g/7 oz. toor dhal
750 ml/3¼ cups boiling water
½ tsp fine sea salt
½ tsp ground turmeric

TADKA

3 tbsp vegetable oil
2 cloves
2 cardamom pods
½ tsp cumin seeds
½ tsp mustard seeds
1 onion, finely chopped
½ tsp fine sea salt
1 tsp garlic paste
1 tsp ginger paste
½ tsp ground cumin
½ tsp ground coriander
½ tsp ground turmeric
½ tsp Kashmiri chilli/chili powder
3 medium tomatoes, chopped
1 tsp palm sugar/jaggery

TO FINISH

125 ml/½ cup natural/plain yogurt
200 ml/generous ¾ cup boiling water
1 tsp garam masala
5–7 fresh coriander/cilantro stems, roughly chopped

SPICED MATOKI

2 matoki (yellow plantain)
¼ tsp Himalayan sea salt
¼ tsp freshly ground black pepper
¼ tsp amchoor (dried mango powder)
50 ml/3½ tbsp vegetable oil

pressure cooker (optional)

SERVES 5

For the dhal base, pick through the toor dhal to remove any stones. Place it in a colander and rinse under cold running water until the water runs clear. Transfer the rinsed lentils to a pressure cooker with the boiling water, salt and turmeric. Close the pressure cooker and place over a medium heat. Cook for about 15 minutes or 9 whistles. (If you don't have a pressure cooker, you will first need to soak the picked and rinsed lentils in 1 litre/quart of boiling water for 4–5 hours. Drain, then transfer the lentils to a large saucepan with 1 litre/quart of fresh boiling water, the salt and turmeric. Cover with a lid and bring to the boil, then simmer over a medium heat for 60–70 minutes, topping up the boiling water as needed.)

Towards the end of the lentil cooking time, prepare the tadka. Put the vegetable oil into a saucepan over a medium heat. Add the cloves and cardamom pods and fry for 20 seconds until they have released their aromas into the hot oil. Add the cumin and mustard seeds and fry, gently shaking the pan, until the seeds have sizzled and popped. Add the onion and salt and fry for 7–8 minutes, or until the onions are softened and lightly browned. Stir in the garlic and ginger pastes and fry for 1 minute. Stir in the ground cumin, coriander, turmeric and Kashmiri chilli/chili powder and fry for another minute. Add the chopped tomatoes and palm sugar/jaggery. Cover the pan with a lid and cook for 5 minutes, until the tomatoes have softened.

Meanwhile, when the lentils are cooked (they should be soft and falling apart), release the steam from the pressure cooker slowly (or remove the pan from the heat). Most of the water should have been absorbed during cooking, but gently crush the lentils with any small amount that remains.

Add the yogurt to the simmering tomato mixture, followed by the cooked toor dhal and the extra boiling water (adding more or less depending on how you prefer the consistency). Stir well and turn the heat down to its lowest setting. Simmer gently for 10–15 minutes while you prepare the matoki.

Peel the matoki and slice them diagonally into approximately 1-cm/½-inch widths.

In a small bowl, mix the Himalayan sea salt with the black pepper and amchoor (dried mango powder) until well combined.

Put the oil into a medium frying pan/skillet over a medium heat. Add the matoki slices to the hot oil and fry for 2–3 minutes on each side until golden brown. Transfer the fried matoki to a plate and dust all over with the Himalayan salt mixture. Set aside.

Check and adjust the seasoning. Stir in the garam masala and chopped coriander/cilantro and remove from the heat. The texture should resemble a smooth lentil soup.

Serve the dhal with the spiced matoki.

SMOKED TOMATO TIKKA MASALA TOOR DHAL

The tikka masala is a British-Indian concoction from the 1970s. Its true origin is hazy, lost in thousands of versions of the 'proper' tikka masala sauce over the years. One thing for certain is that it certainly made an impact, and is still a much-loved dish by many in Britain today. My tikka masala-inspired dhal has always been a crowd-pleaser. What's not to like about soft lentils immersed in a spiced, creamy tomato sauce? What elevates this dish to the next level is the hint of smokiness delivered by the charred whole tomatoes, which are then puréed down, skin, seeds and all! This means zero waste and lots of flavour.

TOOR DHAL BASE

200 g/7 oz. toor dhal
750 ml/3¼ cups boiling water
½ tsp fine sea salt, plus extra to taste
½ tsp ground turmeric

SMOKED TOMATO PURÉE

4 large tomatoes
2 tbsp vegetable oil

TO FINISH

2 tbsp vegetable oil
1 tsp garlic paste
1 tsp ginger paste
½ tsp ground cumin
½ tsp ground coriander
½ tsp ground turmeric
½ tsp Kashmiri chilli/chili powder
1 tsp dried fenugreek leaves
½ tsp fine sea salt
2 tbsp runny honey
1 tbsp ground almonds
1 tbsp ground cashews
100 g/½ cup natural/plain yogurt
115 ml/½ cup single/light cream
1 tsp garam masala
Roti Breads (see page 89) or cooked basmati rice, to serve (optional)

pressure cooker (optional)

SERVES 6

For the dhal base, pick through the toor dhal to remove any stones. Place it in a colander and rinse under cold running water until the water runs clear.

Transfer the rinsed lentils to a pressure cooker with the boiling water, salt and turmeric. Close the pressure cooker and place over a medium heat. Cook for about 15 minutes or 9 whistles. (If you don't have a pressure cooker, you will first need to soak the picked and rinsed lentils in 1 litre/quart of boiling water for 4–5 hours. Drain, then transfer the lentils to a large saucepan with 1 litre/quart of fresh boiling water, the salt and turmeric. Cover with a lid and bring to the boil, then simmer over a medium heat for 60–70 minutes, topping up the boiling water as needed.)

While the dhal is cooking, start to prepare the smoked tomato purée.

Preheat the oven to 180°C (350°F) Gas 4.

Place the whole tomatoes in a roasting pan. Drizzle over the vegetable oil and place the pan in the preheated oven. Roast the tomatoes for 20 minutes, until softened.

Meanwhile, when the lentils are cooked (they should be soft and mashable), release the steam from the pressure cooker slowly (or remove the pan from the heat). Most of the water should have been absorbed during cooking, but gently crush the lentils with any small amount of cooking water that remains and set aside.

Preheat a grill/broiler to high.

Place the roasting pan of softened tomatoes under the hot grill/broiler for about 8 minutes until they are charred and blackened. Purée the charred tomatoes (skin, seeds and all) in a food processor until smooth. Set aside.

To finish the dish, place the vegetable oil in a large saucepan over a medium heat. Add the garlic and ginger pastes and fry in the hot oil for 30 seconds to release the aromas. Add the ground cumin, coriander, turmeric, Kashmiri chilli/chili powder and dried fenugreek leaves and fry with the ginger and garlic for 1 minute. Add the smoked tomato purée and salt and stir into the spices. Simmer the sauce base for 3–4 minutes.

Add the honey, ground almonds, ground cashews, natural/plain yogurt and single/light cream. Stir the sauce well to remove any lumps and simmer for a further 2–3 minutes.

Pour the cooked toor dhal into the tikka sauce mixture, stir well and simmer for a final 3–4 minutes.

Check the seasoning and add more salt to taste, if needed. Stir in the garam masala, and remove the dhal from the heat.

Serve the dhal on its own as a soup or accompanied with roti breads or basmati rice.

TOOR DHAL BASE

150 g/½ cup toor dhal

500 ml/2 cups plus 2 tbsp boiling water

2.5-cm/1-inch piece of fresh ginger, peeled and grated

½ tsp fine sea salt

TADKA

5 tbsp vegetable oil

1-cm/½-inch piece of cassia bark or cinnamon stick

4 cloves

½ tsp mustard seeds

½ tsp cumin seeds

10–15 fresh curry leaves

½ tsp ground cumin

½ tsp ground coriander

½ tsp ground turmeric

½ tsp Kashmiri chilli/chili powder

TO FINISH

200 ml/generous ¾ cup coconut milk

1 tsp palm sugar/jaggery

50 g/1¾ oz. chopped fresh kale

TO SERVE

dried coconut chips

cooked basmati rice or Naan Breads (see page 108)

pressure cooker (optional)

SERVES 4

COCONUT AND KALE TOOR DHAL

Here, sweet, nutty coconut milk is added to the toor dhal base alongside the spiced seasoned oil. Super-healthy kale and coconut chips bring an extra dimension of texture.

For the dhal base, pick through the toor dhal to remove any stones. Place it in a colander and rinse under cold running water until the water runs clear. Transfer the rinsed lentils to a pressure cooker with the boiling water, ginger and salt. Close the pressure cooker and place over a medium heat. Cook for about 15 minutes or 9 whistles. (If you don't have a pressure cooker, you will first need to soak the picked and rinsed lentils in 1 litre/quart of boiling water for 4–5 hours. Drain, then transfer the lentils to a large saucepan with 1 litre/quart of fresh boiling water, the ginger and salt. Cover with a lid and bring to the boil, then simmer over a medium heat for 60–70 minutes, topping up the boiling water as needed.)

When the lentils are soft and falling apart, release the steam from the pressure cooker slowly (or remove the pan from the heat). Most of the water should have been absorbed during cooking, but gently crush the lentils with any small amount that remains. Set aside.

For the tadka, place the vegetable oil in a large saucepan over a medium heat. Add the cassia bark or cinnamon stick and the cloves and let them sizzle for 30 seconds. Add the mustard and cumin seeds and shake the pan gently. After about 30 seconds, stir in the curry leaves, cumin, coriander, turmeric and Kashmiri chilli/chili powder.

Pour the cooked toor dhal base into the seasoned oil and mix well. Simmer gently over a medium heat for 2–3 minutes.

To finish, pour in the coconut milk, add the palm sugar/jaggery and kale. Simmer gently for 10 minutes to allow the kale to soften.

Meanwhile, toast the coconut chips in a hot, dry frying pan/skillet for 2–3 minutes, stirring constantly, until crisp and toasted.

Divide the dhal into serving bowls and top each one with toasted coconut chips. Serve on its own or with cooked rice or naan breads.

SOUTH INDIAN SAMBHAR DHAL

With a freshly ground, pungent sambhar masala spice blend, this dhal packs a serious punch of flavour. The spice blend recipe here makes more than is needed for this dish. Store the leftover masala in an airtight jar in a cool, dark place for up to 3 months

SAMBHAR MASALA

½ tbsp coriander seeds
½ tbsp cumin seeds
½ tbsp mustard seeds
½ tbsp whole black peppercorns
½ tbsp split channa dhal, picked
½ tbsp split white urad dhal, picked
10 fresh curry leaves
1 dried long red chilli/chile
¼ tsp asafoetida powder
¼ tsp ground turmeric

SAMBHAR DHAL BASE

125 g/4½ oz. toor dhal
750 ml/3¼ cups boiling water
½ tsp ground turmeric
½ tsp fine sea salt

SAMBHAR VEGETABLES

4 tbsp vegetable oil
1 onion, chopped
pinch of fine sea salt
30 g/1 oz. fresh ginger, peeled and grated
1 tsp Sambhar Masala (see left)
1 carrot, peeled and chopped into 2.5-cm/1-inch chunks
2 medium tomatoes, roughly chopped
2 tsp palm sugar/jaggery
1 small aubergine/eggplant, chopped into 2.5-cm/1-inch chunks
100 g/3½ oz. green beans, topped and tailed and halved
200 ml/generous ¾ cup boiling water

TO FINISH

½ tsp tamarind paste
2 tsp palm sugar/jaggery
5–6 fresh coriander/cilantro stems, roughly chopped
cooked basmati rice or Roti Breads (see page 89), to serve

TADKA

3 tbsp vegetable oil
1 tsp cumin seeds
1 tsp mustard seeds
1 green chilli/chile, slit in half lengthways
10–12 fresh curry leaves
pinch of asafoetida powder

pressure cooker (optional)

SERVES 4

For the sambhar dhal base, pick through the toor dhal to remove any stones. Place it in a colander and rinse under cold running water until the water runs clear. Transfer the washed lentils to a pressure cooker with the boiling water, the turmeric and salt. Close the pressure cooker and place over a medium heat. Cook for about 10–12 minutes or 6–7 whistles. (If you don't have a pressure cooker, you will first need to soak the lentils in 1 litre/ quart of boiling water for 3–4 hours. Drain, then transfer the lentils to a large saucepan with 750 ml/3¼ cups of fresh boiling water, the turmeric and salt. Cover with a lid and bring to the boil, then simmer over a medium heat for 60–70 minutes, topping up the boiling water as needed.)

Meanwhile, for the sambhar masala, place a dry frying pan/skillet over a medium-high heat and add the coriander seeds, cumin seeds, mustard seeds, whole peppercorns, split channa dhal and split white urad dhal. Toast the spices, shaking the pan constantly, for 2–3 minutes. Add the fresh curry leaves, dried chillies/chiles, asafoetida powder and turmeric and toast for a further 30 seconds, still shaking the pan. Transfer the mixture to a spice or coffee grinder or pestle and mortar and blitz to a coarse powder. Set aside.

Towards the end of the lentil cooking time, place the vegetable oil for the sambhar vegetables in a large saucepan over a medium heat. Add the onion and salt and fry for 7–8 minutes until golden. Add the ginger and fry for 1 minute. Add the 1 teaspoon of sambhar masala, mix with the onion and fry for 1 minute. If the pan starts to dry out, add a splash of boiling water. Add the carrot, mix well and fry for 4 minutes. Add the tomatoes and the palm sugar/jaggery. Cover the pan with a lid and fry for 5 minutes until the tomatoes have started to soften. Add the aubergine/eggplant and fry for 5 minutes.

Meanwhile, when the lentils are soft, release the steam from the pressure cooker slowly (or remove the pan from the heat). Most of the water should have been absorbed, but gently crush the lentils with any that remains.

Stir the cooked lentils into the sambhar vegetables. Simmer for 5 minutes. Add the green beans and boiling water. Stir and turn the heat down to low. Simmer for 12–15 minutes until the vegetables have softened.

Stir in the tamarind paste, palm sugar/ jaggery and coriander/cilantro. Simmer for a few minutes while you make the tadka.

For the tadka, put the vegetable oil into a small saucepan over a medium heat and add the cumin and mustard seeds. Fry for 1 minute, then mix in the chilli/chile, curry leaves and asafoetida powder. Tip everything into the sambhar and stir well. Serve the sambhar with cooked rice or roti breads.

MASOOR DHAL

Also known as split red lentils, masoor dhal is absolutely packed with nutrients, especially being abundantly rich in iron and protein. Its powerful health benefits have been recognized for centuries, which is why it is such an important part of Indian cuisine. Masoor dhal also carries the reputation of being the most delicious and flavoursome of all the lentils, owing to its natural hint of sweetness. This inexpensive dhal is quite easy to prepare – it does not need soaking and is quick to cook compared to other legumes – 20 minutes of simmering and you are done – so choose a recipe from this chapter if you are short on time. Masoor dhal tends to be my personal choice for lentil soups, as I find that it doesn't thicken up as much as the other lentils do, which is great for when you're making a bulk amount of soup to feed a crowd!

MASOOR DHAL AND ROASTED BEETROOT DHANSAK

This dish has elements of Persian and Gujarati cookery. Traditionally the dhansak is a lamb-based dish, however, this recipe makes for a delicious vegetarian alternative.

ROASTED BEETROOT

450 g/1 lb. raw beetroot/beet, peeled and chopped into 1-cm/½-inch chunks
1 tbsp desiccated/dried shredded coconut
2 tbsp olive oil
½ tsp fine sea salt

MASOOR DHAL

2 tbsp ghee (or butter)
1 tsp cumin seeds
1 onion, finely diced
small pinch of fine sea salt
2.5-cm/1-inch piece of fresh ginger, peeled and finely grated
½ tsp Kashmiri chilli/chili powder
½ tsp ground cumin
½ tsp ground coriander
½ tsp ground turmeric
50 ml/3½ tbsp boiling water
2 medium tomatoes, roughly chopped
200 g/7 oz. masoor dhal
1 litre/quart boiling water
½ tsp garam masala
5–6 fresh coriander/cilantro stems
cooked basmati rice and Cucumber Raita (see page 89), to serve

baking sheet, lined with baking parchment

SERVES 4

Preheat the oven to 170°C (340°F) Gas 3.

Place the beetroot/beet in a mixing bowl with the desiccated/dried shredded coconut, the oil and salt. Toss well. Transfer the beets to the prepared baking sheet and roast in the preheated oven for 30 minutes, turning halfway through, until softened and browned.

Meanwhile, for the masoor dhal base. Put the ghee (or butter) into a saucepan over a medium heat. Add the cumin seeds and let them sizzle for 1 minute. Add the onion and salt and fry for 8–10 minutes, until softened and lightly browned.

Stir in the ginger and fry for 1 minute. Add the Kashmiri chilli/chili powder, cumin, coriander and turmeric and fry for 30 seconds. Immediately pour in the 50 ml/3½ tablespoons of boiling water to loosen the ingredients and prevent the spices from catching. Turn the heat down to low and simmer gently for 2 minutes. Stir in the tomatoes and allow them to soften and melt for 2–3 minutes.

Meanwhile, pick through the masoor dhal to remove any stones, then rinse under cold running water and drain well. Add the lentils to the pan, then pour in the 1 litre/quart of boiling water. Stir well and allow the dhal to simmer for 20 minutes over a low-medium heat, stirring occasionally.

Tip half of the roasted beetroot/beet into the dhansak and keep the remainder warm in a low oven for the garnish. Simmer the dhansak over a low heat, uncovered, for a further 5–6 minutes until reduced and thickened.

Stir through the garam masala and coriander/cilantro and warm through for 1 last minute. Serve topped with the remaining roasted beetroot/beet and some cooked basmati rice and cucumber raita.

SIMPLE GINGERY MASOOR DHAL

MASOOR DHAL

2 tbsp vegetable oil
1 onion, chopped
½ tsp fine sea salt
1 tbsp peeled and grated fresh ginger
½ tsp ground turmeric
½ tsp ground cumin
½ tsp ground coriander
¼ tsp freshly ground black pepper
2 medium tomatoes, roughly chopped
200 g/7 oz. masoor dhal
1 litre/quart boiling water
½ tsp garam masala
5–6 fresh coriander/cilantro stems, roughly chopped
Roti Breads (see page 89) or cooked basmati rice, to serve (optional)

TADKA

3 tbsp vegetable oil
½ tsp cumin seeds
½ tsp mustard seeds
1 tbsp peeled and grated fresh ginger

SERVES 6

There is much ayurvedic influence in Indian cuisine – the ancient 'science of life' that promotes health through our diets. It's 'feel-good dishes' like my warming gingery masoor dhal that add substance to this theory.

For the dhal base, put the vegetable oil into a large saucepan over a medium heat. Add the onion and salt and fry for about 8–9 minutes until the onion is softened and lightly browned.

Stir in the grated ginger and fry for 1 minute. Add the turmeric, cumin, coriander and black pepper and mix well to coat the onion in the spices. Tip in the chopped tomatoes and fry for 2 minutes.

Meanwhile, pick through the masoor dhal to remove any stones, then rinse under cold running water and drain well. Stir the lentils into the onion and tomatoes and fry for 1 minute. Add the boiling water and simmer the dhal for 20 minutes, until the lentils are mushy and the mixture has reduced by a third.

Remove from the heat and blend the dhal with a stick blender or in a food processor to the texture of a smooth soup. Return the dhal to the pan over a medium heat. Stir in the garam masala and coriander/cilantro and let the dhal simmer for 2–3 minutes while you make the tadka.

Place the vegetable oil in a small saucepan over a medium heat. Add the cumin and mustard seeds and let them sizzle in the hot oil for 1 minute. Add the grated ginger and fry for 20 seconds. Pour the hot tadka oil into the dhal base and stir well.

Remove the dhal from the heat and rest for 2 minutes before serving on its own or with roti breads or cooked rice.

SIMPLE SPINACH MASOOR DHAL

Versatile spinach is the magic ingredient here – when puréed together with the sweet red lentils, it creates a buttery texture, very typical of North Indian cuisine.

MASOOR DHAL

2 tbsp vegetable oil
1 onion, chopped
½ tsp fine sea salt
1 tbsp peeled and grated fresh ginger
2 garlic cloves, grated
½ tsp ground turmeric
½ tsp ground cumin
½ tsp ground coriander
¼ tsp Kashmiri chilli/chili powder
2 medium tomatoes, roughly chopped
200 g/7 oz. masoor dhal
1 litre/quart boiling water
½ tsp garam masala
1 tsp palm sugar/jaggery
Roti Breads (see page 89) or cooked basmati rice, to serve (optional)

WILTED SPINACH

2 tbsp mustard seed oil
200 g/7 oz. fresh baby spinach
pinch of fine sea salt

TADKA

2 tbsp vegetable oil
2 cloves
2 cardamom pods
½ tsp cumin seeds
½ tsp mustard seeds

SERVES 6-8

For the dhal base, put the vegetable oil into a large saucepan over a medium heat. Add the onion and salt and fry for about 8–9 minutes until the onion is softened and lightly browned.

Stir in the grated ginger and garlic and fry for 2 minutes. Add the turmeric, cumin, coriander and chilli/chili powder and mix well. Tip in the chopped tomatoes and fry for 2 minutes.

Meanwhile, pick through the masoor dhal to remove any stones, then rinse under cold running water and drain well. Stir the lentils into the onion and tomatoes and fry for 1 minute. Add the boiling water and simmer the dhal for 20 minutes, until reduced and the lentils are falling apart.

While this is cooking, put the mustard seed oil into a frying pan/skillet over a medium heat. Add the spinach and salt and fry for 1–2 minutes until wilted. Stir the wilted spinach into the dhal. Remove the dhal from the heat and blend with a stick blender or in a food processor to the texture of a smooth soup.

Return the dhal to the pan over a medium heat and stir in the garam masala and palm sugar/jaggery. Simmer over a very low heat for 2–3 minutes whilst you prepare the tadka.

Place the vegetable oil into a small saucepan over a medium heat. Add the cloves and cardamom pods and fry for 20 seconds. Add the cumin and mustard seeds and fry for 1 minute, or until they sizzle and crackle. Pour the tadka oil into the dhal and stir.

Simmer the dhal over a low heat for 1 final minute before serving on its own or with roti breads or cooked rice.

MASOOR DHAL
2 tbsp vegetable oil
2 cloves
2 cardamom pods
2.5-cm/1-inch piece of cassia bark or cinnamon stick
½ tsp cumin seeds
½ tsp mustard seeds
1 onion, chopped
½ tsp fine sea salt
1 tbsp peeled and grated fresh ginger
2 garlic cloves, grated
½ tsp ground turmeric
½ tsp ground cumin
½ tsp ground coriander
¼ tsp Kashmiri chilli/chili powder
2 medium tomatoes, roughly chopped
1 tsp palm sugar/jaggery
200 g/7 oz. masoor dhal
1 litre/quart boiling water
½ tsp garam masala
5–6 fresh coriander/cilantro stems, roughly chopped

BROCCOLI
200 g/7 oz. tenderstem broccoli, trimmed
2 tbsp vegetable oil
¼ tsp sea salt flakes
¼ tsp coarsely cracked black pepper
¼ tsp dried chilli flakes/hot red pepper flakes, plus extra to serve

SERVES 5

MASOOR DHAL WITH TENDERSTEM BROCCOLI

Roasted, seasoned and spiced broccoli brings wonderful natural sweetness and texture to this wholesome sea of flavoursome dhal. It's so simple, yet utterly delicious.

Preheat the oven to 180°C (350°F) Gas 4.

For the masoor dhal base, put the vegetable oil into a saucepan over a medium heat. Add the cloves, cardamom pods and cassia or cinnamon stick and fry for 20 seconds until they have released their aroma into the hot oil. Add the cumin and mustard seeds and fry, while gently shaking the pan, for 20 seconds until the seeds have sizzled and popped. Add the onion and salt and fry in the spiced oil for 7–8 minutes until the onion is soft and lightly browned.

Stir in the grated ginger and garlic and fry for 1 minute. Add the turmeric, cumin, coriander and Kashmiri chilli/chili powder and mix well to coat the onion in the spices. Add the chopped tomatoes and palm sugar/jaggery and fry for 4 minutes.

Meanwhile, pick through the masoor dhal to remove any stones, then rinse under cold running water and drain well. Stir the washed lentils into the onion and tomato base and fry for 1 minute. Pour in the boiling water and simmer for 20 minutes over a medium heat, until the lentils are falling apart and the water has been absorbed.

While the dhal is simmering, cut any larger stems of broccoli in half and place in a roasting pan. Drizzle over the oil and sprinkle over the sea salt, cracked black pepper and dried chilli flakes/hot red pepper flakes. Toss the broccoli in the oil. Roast the broccoli in the preheated oven for 12 minutes or until slightly softened and charred.

When the lentils are cooked, stir in the garam masala and chopped coriander/cilantro and simmer for 1 final minute.

Divide the dhal between serving bowls and top with the roasted broccoli. Serve with extra chilli flakes/hot red pepper flakes, if liked.

MASOOR DHAL AND ROASTED SWEET POTATO

Here, I've roasted sweet potato in a blend of punchy spices and coarsely chopped pistachio nuts. These jewel-like chunks of potato top a hearty and flavoursome fried onion and tomato based masoor dhal. With cumin seeds, mustard seeds and curry leaves packing a pungent punch, the garam masala spice and fresh coriander/cilantro beautifully round off this supremely comforting dish.

MASOOR DHAL

2 tbsp vegetable oil
2 cloves
2 cardamom pods
2.5-cm/1-inch piece of cassia bark or cinnamon stick
½ tsp cumin seeds
½ tsp mustard seeds
10–15 fresh curry leaves
1 onion, chopped
½ tsp fine sea salt
1 tbsp peeled and grated fresh ginger
2 garlic cloves, grated
½ tsp ground turmeric
½ tsp ground cumin
½ tsp ground coriander
¼ tsp Kashmiri chilli/chili powder
2 medium tomatoes, roughly chopped
200 g/7 oz. masoor dhal
1 litre/quart boiling water
½ tsp garam masala
5–6 fresh coriander/cilantro stems, roughly chopped

SWEET POTATO

1 sweet potato, peeled and chopped into 2.5-cm/1-inch chunks
2 tbsp vegetable oil
¼ tsp sea salt flakes
¼ tsp dried chilli flakes/hot red pepper flakes
¼ tsp coarsely cracked black pepper
1 tbsp chopped pistachios

SERVES 6-8

Preheat the oven to 160°C (325°F) Gas 3.

For the sweet potato, place the peeled and chopped sweet potato in a roasting pan and drizzle over the vegetable oil. Sprinkle over the sea salt, dried chilli flakes/hot red pepper flakes and cracked black pepper and toss everything together. Roast the sweet potato in the preheated oven for 30 minutes until soft, checking and turning every 10 minutes.

While the potato chunks are roasting, prepare the masoor dhal base. Put the vegetable oil into a large saucepan over a medium heat. Add the cloves, cardamom pods and cassia bark or cinnamon stick and fry for 20 seconds until they have released their aromas into the hot oil. Add the cumin and mustard seeds and fry for 20 seconds, or until the seeds have sizzled and popped. Add the fresh curry leaves and gently shake the pan to ensure all of the ingredients are evenly distributed. Add the chopped onion and salt and fry for 7–8 minutes, or until the onion is softened and lightly browned.

Stir in the grated ginger and garlic and fry with the onion for 1 minute. Next, add the turmeric, cumin, coriander and Kashmiri chilli/chili powder and mix well to coat the onion in the spices. Stir in the chopped tomatoes and fry for 2 minutes.

Meanwhile, pick through the masoor dhal to remove any stones, then rinse under cold running water and drain well. Add the washed lentils and mix into the onion and tomato. Cook for 1 minute.

Carefully pour in the boiling water and allow the mixture to simmer for 20 minutes over a medium heat, or until the lentils have softened to the extent that they are mushy and falling apart.

By now the sweet potato should be roasted and softened too, so remove the pan from the oven and sprinkle over the chopped pistachios. Roast for a final 5 minutes.

Once the lentils are cooked and the dhal has thickened and reduced, sprinkle over the garam masala and chopped coriander/cilantro and stir in well.

Divide the dhal between serving bowls and serve topped with the roasted sweet potato chunks.

CHANNA DHAL

Channa dhal is the Gujarati term for the more commonly known chickpeas or garbanzo beans. There are two main types of chickpeas; white and brown. The white variety of chickpeas is more popular in the West, whereas the brown variety is more traditional to Indian cuisine. Brown chickpeas are slightly smaller and have more of a nutty depth of flavour. It is the raw brown chickpeas, which are dried, de-husked and then split that give the dhal form. Channa dhal is high in fibre and protein, and like all dhals, is low in fat. Upon cooking until soft, channa dhal delivers a rich and slightly pappy consistency, however, due to its pleasant nuttiness, channa dhal is often cooked until soft but still retaining its shape, so that the unique texture and taste can be enjoyed.

CHANNA DHAL WITH CHARRED STICKY PANEER OR TOFU

In this recipe, the channa dhal is cooked with turmeric until soft, then submerged in a spiced, fragrant sauce. Buttery-soft onions, fresh ginger, garlic, green chilli/chile and a blend of aromatic spices and tomatoes are simmered down together to give the perfect balance of spice, sweet and sourness. For the topping, choose between chunks of roasted paneer, marinated in a sweet and sticky tamarind glaze, or chunks of charred marinated sticky tofu for a vegan option.

CHANNA DHAL BASE

150 g/5½ oz. channa dhal
½ tsp fine sea salt
½ tsp ground turmeric
1 litre/quart boiling water

TADKA

3 tbsp vegetable oil
1 tsp cumin seeds
4 garlic cloves, thinly sliced
25 g/1 oz. piece of fresh ginger, peeled and grated
1 green chilli/chile, halved lengthways
10–12 fresh curry leaves
pinch of asafoetida powder
1 onion, finely chopped
½ tsp fine sea salt
½ tsp ground cumin
½ tsp ground coriander
½ tsp ground turmeric

TO FINISH

2 large tomatoes, roughly chopped
1 tsp palm sugar/jaggery
freshly squeezed juice of ½ lemon
5–6 fresh coriander/cilantro stems, plus extra to garnish (optional)
Charred Sticky Paneer or Charred Sticky Tofu (see page 40), to serve

pressure cooker (optional)

SERVES 4

For the channa dhal base, pick through the dhal to remove any stones. Place it in a colander and rinse under cold running water until the water runs clear.

Place the washed dhal in a pressure cooker along with the salt, turmeric and boiling water. Close the pressure cooker and place over a medium heat. Cook for about 15 minutes or 9 whistles. (If you don't have a pressure cooker, you will first need to soak the picked and rinsed lentils in 1 litre/quart of boiling water for 3–4 hours. Drain, then transfer the lentils to a large saucepan with 1 litre/quart of fresh boiling water, the salt and turmeric. Cover with a lid, bring to the boil and then simmer over a medium heat for 45 minutes, topping up with more boiling water as needed.)

When cooked, the lentils should be soft but should still hold their round disc-like shape. Release the steam from the pressure cooker slowly (or remove the pan from the heat). Remove the lentils, and drain and reserve the cooking water. Set both aside until needed.

Next, prepare the tadka. Put the vegetable oil into a saucepan over a medium heat. Add the cumin seeds and allow them to sizzle and crackle in the hot oil for 1 minute. Add the sliced garlic, grated ginger, green chilli/chile and fresh curry leaves. Gently shake the pan, so that all of the ingredients are coated in the oil and fry for 30 seconds. Add the asafoetida powder and shake the pan once more. Add the chopped onion and salt and fry for 10 minutes until the onion is softened and lightly browned.

Add the cumin, coriander and turmeric. Stir well to coat the onion in the spices and fry for 30 seconds. If the pan dries out, add a splash of the reserved lentil cooking water to loosen the ingredients and stop them from sticking to the bottom of the pan.

Stir in the chopped tomatoes, then reduce the heat to low and allow the tomatoes to soften and completely melt for 5–6 minutes. Keep stirring to ensure the tomatoes do not stick to the pan.

Once the tomatoes have completely melted down to form a sauce base, add the palm sugar/jaggery, the cooked channa dhal and the lemon juice. Mix well and simmer gently for a further 6–7 minutes.

Add the chopped coriander/cilantroto finish and mix in well. Remove from the heat and divide the channa dhal between serving bowls. Top with the charred sticky chunks of paneer or tofu, as you prefer, and garnish with extra coriander/cilantro to serve, if liked.

CHARRED STICKY PANEER

200 g/7 oz. diced paneer
1 tbsp vegetable oil
½ tbsp tamarind paste
1 tsp palm sugar/ jaggery

baking sheet, lined with baking parchment

SERVES 4
AS A TOPPING

Preheat the oven to 180°C (350°F) Gas 4.

Place the diced paneer in a mixing bowl and add the vegetable oil, tamarind paste and palm sugar/ jaggery. Mix well to evenly coat the paneer in the marinade. Space out the paneer on the prepared baking sheet and roast in the preheated oven for 12 minutes until slightly charred and crisp. Keep warm until needed.

CHARRED STICKY TOFU

200 g/7 oz. diced firm tofu
1 tbsp vegetable oil
½ tbsp tamarind paste
1 tsp palm sugar/ jaggery

baking sheet, lined with baking parchment

SERVES 4
AS A TOPPING

Preheat the oven to 180°C (350°F) Gas 4.

Place the diced tofu in a mixing bowl and add the vegetable oil, tamarind paste and palm sugar/jaggery. Mix well to evenly coat the tofu in the marinade. Space out the tofu on the prepared baking sheet and roast in the preheated oven for 12 minutes until slightly charred and crisp. Keep warm until needed.

CHANNA MASALA WITH AUBERGINE

Baingan, ringan, aubergine, eggplant – whatever you call it, one thing is for sure, there is nothing quite like it! Aubergine is great in stews, roasted or even puréed down to make a dip. In this dish, chunks of it are quickly fried in a spiced oil with fragrant curry leaves, then roasted until soft and velvety. This is served atop a flavoursome, aromatic channa masala.

CHANNA DHAL BASE

150 g/5½ oz. channa dhal, picked and rinsed, then soaked in 1 litre/quart boiling water overnight
½ tsp fine sea salt
½ tsp coarsely cracked black pepper

MASALA SAUCE

2 tbsp vegetable oil
1 onion, chopped
½ tsp fine sea salt
1 tsp Holy Trinity Paste (see page 13)
¼ tsp ground turmeric
½ tsp ground cumin
½ tsp ground coriander
2 large tomatoes, roughly chopped
1 tsp palm sugar/jaggery
1 tsp garam masala
5–6 fresh coriander/cilantro stems, roughly chopped

TADKA AUBERGINE

3 tbsp vegetable oil
½ tsp coarsely crushed cumin seeds
½ tsp coarsely crushed coriander seeds
15 fresh curry leaves
1 aubergine/eggplant, chopped into 2.5-cm/1-inch chunks

TADKA

2 tbsp vegetable oil
2 cloves
2 cardamom pods
2.5-cm/1-inch piece of cassia bark or cinnamon stick
½ tsp cumin seeds
½ tsp mustard seeds

SERVES 4-5

Preheat the oven to 180°C (350°F) Gas 4.

Start by preparing the tadka aubergine/eggplant. Put the vegetable oil into a saucepan over a medium heat. Add the crushed cumin and coriander seeds and fry in the hot oil for 30 seconds until sizzling. Add the fresh curry leaves and fry for a further 20 seconds. Carefully tip the diced aubergine/eggplant into the spiced oil and season with the salt and cracked black pepper. Toss the pan so that the aubergine/eggplant chunks are well coated and fry for 2–3 minutes.

Transfer the sealed aubergine/eggplant, along with all the spices and curry leaves, to a roasting pan and roast in the preheated oven for about 20 minutes or until softened. Once roasted, set aside until needed.

Meanwhile, for the channa masala, put the vegetable oil into a large saucepan and add the chopped onion and salt. Fry for 7–8 minutes or until the onion is softened and golden brown.

Stir the holy trinity paste into the onion and fry for 1 minute. Add the turmeric, cumin and coriander and mix well to coat the onion in the spices. Add the chopped tomatoes and palm sugar/jaggery. Turn the heat down to low and fry the tomatoes gently for 5 minutes, or until they have softened and melted down completely. By now, you should be left with a reduced and thickened curry sauce base.

Drain the channa dhal but keep 200 ml/generous 3/4 cup of the soaking water. Add the soaked channa dhal and reserved soaking water to the sauce base, stir together and simmer gently for 20 minutes. The final consistency should be thick and pulpy with the channa still retaining their shape.

While the dhal is simmering, prepare the spiced tadka oil to finish the dish. Put the vegetable oil into a small saucepan and add the cloves, cardamom pods and cassia bark or cinnamon stick. Fry in the hot oil for 20 seconds until the spices have released their natural aromas. Add the cumin and mustard seeds and fry for 20 seconds until they crackle and sizzle in the hot oil. Carefully pour the hot seasoned oil into the dhal base. Stir in the garam masala and chopped coriander/cilantro and simmer for 1 last minute.

Divide the hot dhal between serving bowls and top with the roasted aubergine/eggplant to serve.

CHANNA DHAL FRITTERS

Channa dhal fritters, or dhal vadas as they are also known, make a great snack or appetizer. They consist of a spiced lentil mixture that is formed into small patties and deep-fried. This recipe showcases just how versatile lentils are – the beauty of these moreish fritters is that the outer layer becomes crispy whilst the inner part remains soft.

200 g/7 oz. channa dhal, picked and rinsed, then soaked in 750 ml/3¼ cups boiling water for 4 hours
½ tsp fine sea salt
1 tsp peeled and grated fresh ginger
1 tsp chopped green chillies/chiles
¼ tsp asafoetida powder
½ tsp ground turmeric
5–6 fresh coriander/cilantro stems, roughly chopped
¼ onion, finely chopped
vegetable oil, for deep-frying, plus extra for greasing
Coconut or Hariyali Chutney (see page 13), to serve

MAKES 10

Drain the soaked dhal and discard the soaking water. Remove 2 heaped tablespoons of the soaked dhal and set aside in a bowl until required.

Using a food processor, blitz together the remaining channa dhal until all of the lentils are coarsely blended and form a paste. Add up to 5 tablespoons of cold water (one at a time) while the mixture is blending, if needed, to help process the mixture. Set aside.

Heat the vegetable oil for deep-frying in a deep-fat fryer or large, heavy-based saucepan to 180°C (350°F).

Meanwhile, transfer the blended lentil paste to a mixing bowl and add all the rest of the ingredients, including the reserved whole dhal. Mix well to form a thick fritter batter.

Grease your hands with a little cold oil and then shape the mixture into 10 equally-sized fritters, roughly about 5–6-cm/2–2½-inches in diameter, 1.5-cm/⅝-inch in height and weighing about 55 g/2 oz. each. A good tip is to shape them into balls to start with, then flatten each one a little between your palms so that they look like patties; slightly thicker in the middle and thinner at the edges.

Check that the oil is hot enough by dropping in a teaspoon of the mixture; if it stays in one lump and rises to the surface, then it means the oil is ready. One by one, carefully lower about half of the fritters into the hot oil, ensuring they are not touching. Don't be tempted to touch the fritters until they have turned golden and sealed all over, otherwise this may cause breakage. Deep-fry the fritters for about 10–12 minutes, turning 4–5 times until they are evenly golden brown and crunchy.

Drain the fritters on paper towels and deep-fry the remaining batch. Serve the fritters warm with coconut or hariyali chutney.

GUJARATI DHAL DHOKLI

This is what people from the Gujarat state of India refer to as 'ultimate comfort food', so much so that it is commonly eaten for breakfast at the weekend! Dhoklis are the Gujarati's version of a British dumpling – thin strips of a spiced, whole-wheat flour dough are boiled, then added to this aromatic tadka dhal and simmered until soft and chewy. I like to cut my dough into the traditional bite-sized diamond or round shapes, but you can use any shape you like with this rustic dish.

CHANNA DHAL BASE

200 g/7 oz. channa dhal
750 ml/3¼ cups boiling water
½ tsp fine sea salt
½ tsp ground turmeric

TADKA

2 tbsp ghee (or butter)
1–2 dried red chillies/chiles
½ tsp cumin seeds
½ tsp mustard seeds
10–15 fresh curry leaves
½ tsp asafoetida powder
2 medium tomatoes, chopped
½ tsp fine sea salt
2 tsp palm sugar/jaggery
½ tsp Kashmiri chilli/chili powder
200 ml/generous ¾ cup boiling water

DHOKLIS

75 g/½ cup medium chapatti/fine ground whole-wheat flour, plus extra for dusting
25 g/4 heaped tbsp chickpea/gram flour
1 tsp fine sea salt
2 tbsp ghee (or butter)
¼ tsp ajwain seeds
¼ tsp ground turmeric
¼ tsp Kashmiri chilli/chili powder
60 ml/¼ cup lukewarm water
500 ml/2 cups plus 2 tbsp boiling water
½ tsp fine sea salt

TO SERVE

5–7 fresh coriander/cilantro stems, roughly chopped
papads (spicy poppadoms) and lime pickle, to serve (optional)

pressure cooker (optional)
round or diamond-shaped cookie cutter, about 3–4-cm/1¼–1½-inches

SERVES 4

Pick through the channa dhal to remove any stones. Place it in a colander and rinse under cold running water until the water runs clear.

Place the washed dhal in a pressure cooker with the boiling water, the salt and turmeric. Close the pressure cooker and place over a medium heat. Cook for about 10–12 minutes or 6–7 whistles. (If you don't have a pressure cooker, you will first need to soak the picked and rinsed lentils in 1 litre/quart of boiling water for 3–4 hours. Drain, then transfer the lentils to a large saucepan with 1.5 litres/quarts of fresh boiling water, the salt and turmeric. Cover with a lid and bring to the boil, then simmer over a medium heat for 45 minutes, topping up the water as needed.)

Meanwhile, prepare the dhoklis. In a mixing bowl, stir together the chapatti flour, chickpea/gram flour, salt, ghee (or butter), ajwain seeds, turmeric and Kashmiri chilli/chili powder. Mix in the lukewarm water with a wooden spoon, bit by bit, then use your hands to bring it together into a dough. The dough should not be too sticky so don't use all the water if you don't need it. Cover the dough with clingfilm/plastic wrap and leave to rest at room temperature for 15 minutes.

When the lentils are soft and most of the water has been absorbed, release the steam from the pressure cooker slowly (or remove the pan from the heat). Whisk the lentils with any remaining cooking water and set aside.

Next make the tadka. Put the ghee (or butter) into a saucepan over a medium heat. Add the dried chillies/chiles and the cumin and mustard seeds and let them sizzle in the hot oil for 20 seconds. Add the fresh curry leaves and asafoetida powder and shake the pan to disperse the ingredients. Stir in the chopped tomatoes, salt, palm sugar/jaggery and Kashmiri chilli/chili powder. Cover the saucepan with a lid and turn the heat down low. Cook for 5 minutes, until the tomatoes are softened and completely melted down.

Pour in the cooked channa dhal followed by the boiling water. Whisk together and leave to simmer over a low heat, stirring occasionally, while you finish the dhoklis.

Fill a separate saucepan half-full with the boiling water (it should come about halfway up the sides) and bring to a rolling boil.

Meanwhile, roll out the dhokli dough on a lightly floured surface to approximately 0.5-mm¼-inch thickness. Use your chosen cutter to cut out bite-sized shapes. Gently lower the dhoklis into the boiling water. Add the salt and boil for 10 minutes – if they start sticking, gently separate them using a spoon.

Transfer the cooked dhoklis to a plate. Whisk the remaining dhokli cooking water (approx. 200 ml/generous ¾ cup) into the dhal and then add the boiled dhoklis. Simmer for a final 5 minutes, stirring gently. The texture should resemble a thick stew.

Sprinkle over the coriander/cilantro and serve with papads and lime pickle, if liked.

DOODHI CHANNA DHAL

CHANNA DHAL BASE

150 g/5½ oz. channa dhal, picked and rinsed, then soaked in 1 litre/quart boiling water overnight

DOODHI CHANNA

2 tbsp vegetable oil
½ tsp mustard seeds
½ tsp cumin seeds
1 onion, chopped
½ tsp fine sea salt
1 tsp Holy Trinity Paste (see page 13)
¼ tsp ground turmeric
½ tsp ground cumin
½ tsp ground coriander
2 large tomatoes, roughly chopped
1 tsp palm sugar/ jaggery
1 doodhi/bottle gourd, peeled and chopped into 1-cm/½-inch chunks
500 ml/2 cups plus 2 tbsp boiling water
1 tsp garam masala
5–6 fresh coriander/ cilantro stems, roughly chopped, plus extra to garnish
Roti Breads (see page 89) and Lemon Pickle (see page 110), to serve

SERVES 5

An everyday vegan favourite in Gujarat, whether served in abundance to a whole family by a proud grandmother, taking centre stage in a thali platter in a bustling restaurant, or lovingly prepared in a tiffin box for an exhausted truck driver by his doting wife, the humble doodhi channa is enough to brighten up anyone's day!

For the doodhi channa, put the vegetable oil into a large saucepan over a medium heat. Add the mustard and cumin seeds and fry in the hot oil for 30 seconds, or until the seeds have sizzled and popped. Add the chopped onion and salt and fry for 7–8 minutes or until the onion is softened and lightly browned.

Add the holy trinity paste, stir into the onion and fry for 1 minute. Sprinkle in the turmeric, cumin and coriander and mix well to coat the onion in the spices. Add the chopped tomatoes and fry for 2–3 minutes until they have softened and melted slightly.

Add the soaked channa dhal along with the water it was soaking in and the palm sugar/jaggery. Mix well to combine the ingredients, then turn the heat down to low, cover with a lid and simmer for 20 minutes, stirring occasionally.

Once cooked, the split channa dhal should be soft, but still retain their disc-like shape. Add the chunks of doodhi/bottle gourd and mix well to allow the doodhi/bottle gourd to soak up the flavours of the sauce base. Pour in the boiling water, stir and simmer with the lid on for a final 20 minutes, stirring occasionally, until the doodhi/gourd is tender.

Finish the dish by stirring in the garam masala and chopped coriander/cilantro and simmering for a final minute.

The final dish should have a thin broth-like sauce with distinguishable split channa dhal and chunks of doodhi/bottle gourd. I like to garnish my doodhi channa with a little extra coriander/cilantro and serve alongside warm roti breads and sharp lemon pickle.

URAD DHAL

Also known as black gram, urad dhal originates in India and is widely used in Punjabi cuisine. It is available in two forms: the whole black urad bean (its natural form) and the de-husked split bean, which is the white lentil. The split white lentil is an integral part of South Indian cuisine – it is ground and used as the base of batter mixes for massively popular delicacies, such as steamed fluffy idlis, dosa pancakes and papads or papadums. The whole black variety of urad dhal is the main ingredient in urad dhal dishes, the most popular being Kaali Dhal (see page 61) – simmered and spiced black lentils, and rich Dhal Makhani (see page 58) – simmered and spiced black lentils with the addition of cream and butter. Though it is delicious in rich dishes, urad dhal itself is highly nutritious – high in protein, carbohydrates and iron. Because of this, it's linked with an ayurvedic lifestyle, the ancient holistic health practice where certain foods promote healing.

URAD DHAL WITH FRESH VEGETABLE SAMBHARO

Rich urad dhal cooked with whole garlic cloves until soft and falling apart is then simmered in a fragrantly spiced tomato sauce, which is smoky from dried fenugreek leaves and warming from garam masala. Once simmered, the rich and silky urad dhal is topped with a fresh stir-fried slaw called sambharo. Choose between a traditional sambharo or a more modern Brussels sprouts and carrot sambharo.

URAD DHAL BASE

225 g/8 oz. urad dhal, picked and rinsed, then soaked in 1.5 litres/quarts lukewarm water for 4 hours
2 whole garlic cloves, peeled
1 tsp fine sea salt, plus extra to taste (optional)

TO FINISH

5 tbsp vegetable oil
1 tbsp ginger paste
1 tbsp garlic paste
1 onion, finely chopped
1 tsp fine sea salt
½ tsp ground coriander
½ tsp ground cumin
½ tsp ground turmeric
¼ tsp Kashmiri chilli/chili powder
50 ml/3½ tbsp boiling water (optional)
1 tsp tomato purée/paste
3 large tomatoes, cores and seeds removed, chopped
1 tsp dried fenugreek leaves
1 tsp garam masala
Brussels Sprouts and Carrot Sambharo or Traditional Sambharo, to serve **(see page 54)**

pressure cooker (optional)

SERVES 4-5

Transfer the soaked urad dhal, along with its soaking water, to a pressure cooker with the garlic cloves and salt. Close the pressure cooker and place over a medium heat. Cook for about 20 minutes or 11 whistles. (If you don't have a pressure cooker, transfer the lentils with their soaking water to a large saucepan with the garlic and salt. Cover with a lid, bring to the boil and then simmer over a medium heat for 1 hour, topping up the boiling water as needed.)

Towards the end of the lentil cooking time, put the vegetable oil into a saucepan over a low-medium heat. Add the ginger and garlic pastes and fry for 30 seconds or until the raw aroma has been cooked off and the shreds begin to separate. Add the chopped onion and salt and fry over a medium heat for 10–12 minutes until the onion is buttery soft and golden brown – this caramelized flavour will carry throughout the whole dish.

Add the ground coriander, cumin, turmeric and Kashmiri chilli/chili powder. Stir to coat the onion in the spices and fry for 30–60 seconds. If the pan gets too dry, add the boiling water and mix well. Stir in the tomato purée/paste and fry for 2 minutes. Add the chopped tomatoes and mix well.

Cover the saucepan with a lid and turn the heat down to low. Allow the tomatoes to soften and melt for 10 minutes, stirring frequently so they don't stick to the pan.

Meanwhile, when the lentils are cooked, release the steam from the pressure cooker slowly (or remove the pan from the heat). Most of the water should have been absorbed during cooking, but gently crush the lentils with any small amount that remains.

Add the cooked urad dhal to the simmering dhal base, check the seasoning and add more salt if required. Mix well and simmer for 5 minutes.

To round off the flavour of the dhal off, stir in the dried fenugreek leaves and garam masala, Cover the pan with a lid and switch the heat off. The dhal flavours will continue to develop in the residual heat inside the pan, so do not remove the lid.

While the dhal is resting, make the sambharo following the instructions on page 54. The tadka oil of the sambharo adds an aromatic dimension of flavour, which will enhance the final flavour of the meal.

To serve, divide the urad dhal between serving bowls and top each portion with a serving of the sambharo in its spiced oil.

4 tbsp vegetable oil
½ tsp mustard seeds
½ tsp cumin seeds
1 tsp peeled and finely diced fresh ginger
½ tsp fennel seeds
300 g/10½ oz. shredded Brussels sprouts
1 carrot, peeled and grated
pinch of fine sea salt
1 tbsp freshly chopped coriander/cilantro, to garnish

BRUSSELS SPROUTS AND CARROT SAMBHARO

Put the vegetable oil into a heavy-based saucepan over a medium heat. Add the mustard seeds. Let them sizzle in the hot oil for 30 seconds, then add the cumin seeds and fry for another 30 seconds until they crackle and pop in the hot oil. Add the diced ginger and fry for 30 seconds, gently shaking the pan to disperse the ingredients.

Add the fennel seeds (no need to wait for these to sizzle), followed by the shredded Brussels sprouts and grated carrot. Mix everything well and stir-fry the vegetables for 5–6 minutes, so that they still retain crunch.

Season with the salt and remove from the heat. Garnish with coriander/cilantro and serve immediately.

4 tbsp vegetable oil
1 teaspoon mustard seeds
1 tsp cumin seeds
1 tsp fenugreek seeds
1 tsp peeled and finely diced fresh ginger
½ tsp finely diced garlic
1 tsp fennel seeds
4 green chillies/chiles, slit in half lengthways
25 fresh curry leaves
350 g/2½ cups grated carrot
425 g/6¾ cups grated cabbage
pinch of fine sea salt

EACH SERVES 4
AS A TOPPING

TRADITIONAL SAMBHARO

Put the vegetable oil into a heavy-based saucepan over a medium heat. Add the mustard seeds. Let them sizzle and crackle in the hot oil for 30 seconds, then add the cumin and fenugreek seeds until they crackle and pop. Add the diced ginger and garlic and fry for 30 seconds, gently shaking the pan to disperse the ingredients.

Add the fennel seeds, chillies/chiles and curry leaves, and mix the whole lot together in the pan. Add the carrot and cabbage and mix well so that the oil coats all of the vegetables. Because this is a stir-fry dish, you don't want to overcook the carrot or cabbage – I keep the pan over medium heat for about 6 minutes, so that the vegetables still have a crunch to them.

Season with the salt, then remove from the heat and serve immediately.

URAD DHAL WITH TADKA SHALLOTS AND BEETROOT

One of my favourites dishes in the book, shallots and grated beetroot/beet are fried in hot oil flavoured with a delicate blend of spices and sweet coconut, which deliciously complements and finishes the rich buttery dhal. All the flavours and textures come together beautifully in mildly explosive harmony.

URAD DHAL BASE

- **225 g/8 oz. urad dhal, picked and rinsed, then soaked in 1.5 litres/quarts lukewarm water for 4 hours**
- **2 whole garlic cloves, peeled**
- **1 tsp fine sea salt, plus extra to taste**

TO FINISH

- **4 tbsp vegetable oil**
- **2 cardamom pods**
- **2 cloves**
- **½ tsp cumin seeds**
- **1 tbsp ginger paste**
- **1 tbsp garlic paste**
- **1 onion, finely chopped**
- **1 tsp fine sea salt**
- **½ tsp ground coriander**
- **½ tsp ground cumin**
- **½ tsp ground turmeric**
- **¼ tsp Kashmiri chilli/chili powder**
- **50 ml/3½ tbsp boiling water (optional)**
- **1 tsp tomato purée/paste**
- **3 large tomatoes, cores and seeds removed, chopped**
- **1 tsp dried fenugreek leaves**
- **1 tsp garam masala**

TADKA SHALLOTS AND BEETROOT/BEET

- **4 tbsp vegetable oil**
- **1 tsp peeled and grated ginger**
- **1 green chilli/chile, thinly sliced**
- **4 echalion/banana shallots, thinly sliced**
- **½ tsp fine sea salt**
- **½ tsp freshly ground black pepper**
- **2 raw beetroot/beet, peeled and grated**
- **1 tbsp desiccated/dried shredded coconut**

pressure cooker (optional)

SERVES 6

Transfer the soaked urad dhal, along with its soaking water, to a pressure cooker with the garlic cloves and salt. Close the pressure cooker and place over a medium heat. Cook for about 20 minutes or 11 whistles. (If you don't have a pressure cooker, you can cook the lentils in a large saucepan with the soaking water, the garlic and salt. Cover with a lid and bring to the boil, then simmer over a medium heat for 1 hour, topping up with boiling water as needed.)

Towards the end of the lentil cooking time, put the vegetable oil into a saucepan over a low-medium heat. Add the cardamom pods and cloves and toss in the hot oil for 20 seconds, then add the cumin seeds and fry for 30 seconds. Add the ginger and garlic pastes and fry for 30 seconds or until the raw aroma has been cooked off and the shreds begin to separate. Add the chopped onion and salt and fry over a medium heat for 10–12 minutes until the onion is buttery soft and golden brown.

Add the coriander, cumin, turmeric and Kashmiri chilli/chili powder. Stir to coat the onion in the spices and fry for 30–60 seconds. If the pan gets too dry, add the boiling water and mix well. Stir in the tomato purée/paste and fry for 2 minutes. Add the chopped tomatoes and mix well. Cover the saucepan with a lid and turn the heat down to low. Allow the tomatoes to soften and melt for 10 minutes, stirring frequently so they don't stick to the pan.

Meanwhile, when the lentils are cooked, release the steam from the pressure cooker slowly (or remove the pan from the heat). Most of the water should have been absorbed during cooking, but gently crush the lentils with any small amount that remains.

Add the cooked urad dhal to the simmering dhal base, check the seasoning and add more salt if required. Simmer for 5 minutes while you prepare the tadka shallots and beetroot/beet.

Put the vegetable oil into a frying pan/skillet over a medium heat. Add the grated ginger and sliced green chilli/chile. Fry for 20 seconds in the hot oil before adding the sliced shallots and the salt and pepper. Fry for 5 minutes, stirring, until just golden. Add the grated beetroot/beet and desiccated/dried shredded coconut and toss together well. Fry for 1 minute before removing from the heat.

Add the dried fenugreek leaves and garam masala to the dhal, stir well, and simmer for 1 final minute. The lentils should be soft and mashable and the dhal should be soup-like.

Serve the urad dhal in bowls topped with the tadka shallots and beetroot/beet mixture.

URAD DHAL MAKHANI

Dhal Makhani can be found just about anywhere in Punjab, a northern state of India. It is passionately made in vast amounts in the fast-paced kitchens of the Golden Temple in Amritsar, and holds a special place in almost everyone's heart in the north of India, where it derives from. With silky smooth, soft lentils bathed in an aromatic spiced sauce, cream and butter are added towards the end of cooking for the famously creamy and indulgent texture. To finish this exquisite dhal, the tadka is made using ghee (clarified butter) and aromatic spices for a final rounding flavour.

URAD DHAL BASE

225 g/8 oz. urad dhal, picked and rinsed, then soaked in 1.5 litres/quarts lukewarm water for 4 hours
2 whole garlic cloves, peeled
1 tsp fine sea salt, plus extra to taste

TO FINISH

4 tbsp vegetable oil
1 tbsp ginger paste
1 tbsp garlic paste
1 onion, finely chopped
1 tsp fine sea salt
½ tsp ground coriander
½ tsp ground cumin
½ tsp ground turmeric
¼ tsp Kashmiri chilli/chili powder
1 tsp dried fenugreek leaves
50 ml/3½ tbsp boiling water (optional)
1 tsp tomato purée/paste
3 large tomatoes, cores and seeds removed, chopped
115 ml/½ cup double/heavy cream
1 tbsp unsalted butter
1 tsp garam masala

TADKA

2 tbsp ghee (or butter)
2 cloves
2 cardamom pods
½ tsp cumin seeds
Naan Breads (see page 108), to serve

pressure cooker (optional)

SERVES 4–5

Transfer the soaked urad dhal, along with its soaking water, to a pressure cooker with the garlic cloves and salt. Close the pressure cooker and place over a medium heat. Cook for about 20 minutes or 11 whistles. (If you don't have a pressure cooker, you can cook the lentils in a large saucepan with the soaking water, garlic and salt. Cover with a lid and bring to the boil, then simmer over a medium heat for 1 hour, topping up with boiling water as needed.)

Towards the end of the lentil cooking time, put the vegetable oil into a saucepan over a low-medium heat. Add the ginger and garlic pastes and fry for 30 seconds until the raw aroma has been cooked off and the shreds are beginning to separate. Add the chopped onion and salt and fry over a medium heat for 10–12 minutes until the onion is buttery soft and golden brown – this caramelized base flavour will carry throughout the whole dish.

Add the coriander, cumin, turmeric, Kashmiri chilli/chili powder and dried fenugreek leaves. Stir to coat the onion in the spices and fry for 30–60 seconds. If the pan gets too dry, add the boiling water and mix well to loosen the ingredients in the pan. Stir in the tomato purée/paste and fry for 2 minutes. Add the chopped tomatoes and mix well. Cover the saucepan with a lid and lower the heat. Allow the tomatoes to soften and melt down for 10 minutes, stirring frequently.

Meanwhile, when the lentils are cooked, release the steam from the pressure cooker slowly (or remove the pan from the heat). Most of the water should have been absorbed during cooking, but gently crush the lentils with any small amount that remains.

Add the cooked urad dhal to the simmering dhal base, check the seasoning and add more salt if required. Simmer for 15 minutes. The lentils themselves should be soft and mashable and the dhal should be soup-like in consistency.

Add the double/heavy cream, butter and garam masala. Turn the heat down to very low and simmer gently for 4–5 minutes while you prepare the tadka.

Put the ghee (or butter) into a small saucepan over a medium heat. When it has melted, add the cloves and cardamom pods and fry for 20 seconds. Add the cumin seeds and let them crackle and sizzle in the hot oil. Carefully pour the hot tadka oil into the dhal makhani and stir well. Remove from the heat and serve with naan breads.

KAALI URAD DHAL

URAD DHAL BASE

225 g/8 oz. urad dhal, picked and rinsed, then soaked in 1.5 litres/quarts lukewarm water for 4 hours
2 whole garlic cloves, peeled
1 tsp fine sea salt

TO FINISH

4 tbsp vegetable oil
3 cloves
3 cardamom pods
2.5-cm/1-inch cinnamon stick
½ tsp cumin seeds
1 tbsp ginger paste
1 tbsp garlic paste
1 onion, finely chopped
1 tsp fine sea salt
1 tsp ground coriander
1 tsp ground cumin
½ tsp ground turmeric
¼ tsp Kashmiri chilli/chili powder
50 ml/3½ tbsp boiling water (optional)
1 tbsp tomato purée/paste
3 large tomatoes, cores and seeds removed, chopped
1 tsp dried fenugreek leaves
1 tsp garam masala
Roti Breads (see page 89), to serve

pressure cooker (optional)

SERVES 4–5

This recipe, right here, is one of my childhood loves. Moreish black urad dhal cooked until soft, silky and velvety, then added to a spiced tomato sauce with bags of flavour.

Transfer the soaked urad dhal, along with its soaking water, to a pressure cooker with the garlic cloves and salt. Close the pressure cooker and place over a medium heat. Cook for about 20 minutes or 11 whistles. (If you don't have a pressure cooker, you can cook the lentils in a large saucepan with the soaking water, garlic and salt. Cover with a lid and bring to the boil, then simmer over a medium heat for 1 hour, topping up with boiling water as needed.)

While the lentils are cooking, put the vegetable oil into a saucepan over a low-medium heat. Add the cloves, cardamom pods and cinnamon stick and toss in the hot oil for 20 seconds. Add the cumin seeds and fry for 30 seconds. Add the ginger and garlic pastes and fry for 30 seconds until the raw aroma has gone. Add the onion and salt and fry over a medium heat for 10–12 minutes until the onion becomes buttery soft and golden brown.

Add the ground coriander, cumin, turmeric and Kashmiri chilli/chili powder. Stir to coat the onion in the spices and fry for 30–60 seconds. If the pan gets too dry, add the boiling water and mix well to loosen the ingredients in the pan. Stir in the tomato purée/paste and fry for 1 minute. Add the chopped tomatoes and mix well. Cover the saucepan with a lid and lower the heat. Allow the tomatoes to soften and melt down for 10 minutes, stirring frequently.

Meanwhile, release the steam from the pressure cooker slowly (or remove the pan from the heat). Most of the water should have been absorbed, but crush the lentils with any that remains. Add the urad dhal and mix well, check the seasoning and simmer for 20 minutes.

Stir in the fenugreek leaves and garam masala and simmer for 1 final minute before serving the kaali urad dhal with roti breads.

URAD DHAL WITH METHI AND CHESTNUT MUSHROOOMS

For this delicious dhal, softened, silky and velvety black urad dhal is simmered with a delicately spiced sautéed onion and tomato base. Garlic and ginger pastes bring warming notes and fresh fenugreek leaves deliver an earthy, mildly bitter flavour, complemented by the fragrant heat of garam masala. The richness of this dhal is accompanied by meaty and woody chestnut mushrooms, which are shallow-fried in earthy cumin seeds and ginger paste.

URAD DHAL BASE

225 g/8 oz. urad dhal, picked and rinsed, then soaked in 1.5 litres/quarts lukewarm water for 4 hours
2 whole garlic cloves, peeled
1 tsp fine sea salt, plus extra to taste

TO FINISH

5 tbsp vegetable oil
1 tbsp ginger paste
1 tbsp garlic paste
1 onion, finely chopped
1 tsp fine sea salt
½ tsp ground coriander
½ tsp ground cumin
½ tsp ground turmeric
¼ tsp Kashmiri chilli/chili powder
50 ml/3½ tbsp boiling water
1 tsp tomato purée/paste
3 large tomatoes, chopped
1 tsp palm sugar/jaggery
1 tsp garam masala
100 g/3½ oz. fresh fenugreek, leaves picked off the thicker stems

TADKA CHESTNUT MUSHROOMS

4 tbsp vegetable oil
½ tsp cumin seeds
1 tsp peeled and finely chopped fresh ginger
250 g/9 oz. chestnut mushrooms, sliced
½ tsp fine sea salt

pressure cooker (optional)

SERVES 6

Transfer the soaked urad dhal, along with its soaking water, to a pressure cooker with the garlic cloves and salt. Close the pressure cooker and place over a medium heat. Cook for about 20 minutes or 11 whistles. (If you don't have a pressure cooker, you can cook the lentils in a large saucepan with the soaking water, garlic and salt. Cover with a lid and bring to the boil, then simmer over a medium heat for 1 hour, topping up with boiling water as needed.)

Towards the end of the lentil cooking time, put the vegetable oil into a saucepan over a low-medium heat. Add the ginger and garlic pastes and fry for 30 seconds or until the raw aroma has gone and the shreds begin to separate. Add the onion and salt and fry over a medium heat for 10–12 minutes until the onion is buttery soft and golden brown – this caramelized flavour will carry throughout the whole dish.

Add the ground coriander, cumin, turmeric and Kashmiri chilli/chili powder. Stir to coat the onion in the spices and fry for 30–60 seconds. If the pan gets too dry, add the boiling water and mix well to loosen the ingredients in the pan. Stir in the tomato purée/paste and fry for 2 minutes. Add the chopped tomatoes and palm sugar/jaggery and mix well. Cover the saucepan with a lid, turn the heat down to low and allow the tomatoes to soften and melt down for 10 minutes, stirring frequently.

Meanwhile, when the lentils are cooked, release the steam from the pressure cooker slowly (or remove the pan from the heat). Most of the water should have been absorbed, but gently crush the lentils with any that remains.

Add the cooked lentils to the dhal base and mix well. Check the seasoning and add more salt if required. Simmer for 10 minutes.

Add the garam masala, stir well, cover the dhal with a lid and turn the heat off. The flavours will continue to develop in the residual heat, so don't remove the lid.

Whilst the dhal is resting, make the tadka mushrooms. Put the oil into a heavy-based saucepan over a medium heat. Add the cumin seeds and fry for 30 seconds until they sizzle and pop in the hot oil. Add the ginger and fry for 30 seconds, gently shaking the pan. Add the mushrooms and salt and fry for 3–4 minutes until softened and browned.

Turn the heat back on under the dhal and bring to a gentle boil. Add the fresh fenugreek, stir well and simmer gently for 1 final minute until the leaves have wilted.

Divide the dhal into serving bowls and top each one with some tadka mushrooms.

MOONG DHAL

Moong dhal, also referred to as moong bean, is a favourite legume in Indian cuisine. Thanks to its nutrient credentials it is a classified superfood, though unlike many other lentils it is low in carbohydrates. It is available in two varieties: the whole green moong dhal, or the yellow split moong dhal, which simply has the outer husk removed. The yellow moong dhal is quite neutral in flavour, which makes it the perfect base to take on the flavour of a curry sauce or spiced tadka oil. With the husk removed it is lighter, quicker to cook and does not require such a long soaking time. Most recipes in this chapter use the yellow split moong dhal, apart from the Yogurty Moong Dhal (see page 73), which uses the whole green moong bean – the soaking process takes a bit longer but it gives a unique taste and texture well worth the wait.

MOONG DHAL, KALE AND COCONUT SALAD

200 g/7 oz. yellow split moong dhal, picked and rinsed, then soaked in 1 litre/quart lukewarm water with 1 tsp salt overnight
50 g/1¾ oz. kale, thinly sliced into strips
2 carrots, peeled and grated
½ cucumber, diced into 1-cm/½-inch cubes
2 tbsp desiccated/dried shredded coconut
30 g/1 oz. piece of fresh ginger, peeled and grated
freshly squeezed juice of 1 lime
2 tbsp freshly chopped coriander/cilantro
½ tsp fine sea salt (optional)

TADKA

3 tbsp vegetable oil
1 tsp mustard seeds
pinch of asafoetida powder
15 fresh curry leaves
small pinch of crushed dried chilli flakes/hot red pepper flakes

SERVES 4

Bringing a bit of sunshine to your kitchen, this is a great, light lentil dish to serve in the height of summer. Known in India as Kosambari, it's packed full of flavours and textures very traditional to cuisine from Udupi, a colourful South Indian city. It's traditionally enjoyed during religious festivals.

Drain the soaked moong dhal, discarding the soaking water, and set aside until needed.

Bring a large saucepan of cold water to the boil. Add the kale and boil for 2–3 minutes, then drain into a colander and rinse under cold running water. Drain well again and set aside for a moment.

In a mixing bowl, combine the soaked and drained moong dhal, the grated carrots, diced cucumber, desiccated/dried shredded coconut, grated ginger, lime juice and chopped coriander/cilantro. Add the drained kale and mix all of the ingredients together until well combined. Set aside while you prepare the tadka.

Put the vegetable oil into a small saucepan over a medium heat. Add the mustard seeds and let them sizzle and crackle in the hot oil for 1 minute. Add the asafoetida powder, curry leaves and crushed dried chilli flakes/hot red pepper flakes. Shake the pan well to ensure all the ingredients are coated in oil and then carefully drizzle over the kale salad mixture. Toss well to coat the salad in the seasoned oil and check the seasoning, adding the salt if required. Serve.

MOONG DHAL WITH SPICED ROASTED CAULIFLOWER

Yellow moong dhal is the perfect partner with turmeric and spiced roasted cauliflower – the flavours in this dish deserve a golden medal to go with its golden hue! Naturally sweet and sticky moong dhal is simmered in a spiced velvety tomato sauce and seasoned with a tadka oil infused with earthy cumin seeds and fresh curry leaves – delicious!

MOONG DHAL BASE

150 g/5½ oz. yellow split moong dhal, picked and rinsed, then soaked in 1 litre/quart lukewarm water for 2 hours
½ tsp fine sea salt
½ tsp ground turmeric
1 litre/quart boiling water

TO FINISH

3 tbsp vegetable oil
1 tsp garlic paste
1 tsp ginger paste
3 medium tomatoes, chopped
½ tsp Kashmiri chilli/chili powder
½ tsp ground turmeric
1 tsp garam masala
½ tsp fine sea salt

ROASTED CAULIFLOWER

1 litre/quart boiling water
1 tsp ground turmeric
1 whole cauliflower, cut into florets
3 tbsp vegetable oil
½ tsp coarse sea salt
½ tsp coarsely crushed black pepper
½ tsp cumin seeds
½ tsp crushed coriander seeds
½ tsp chilli flakes/hot red pepper flakes

TADKA

2 tbsp vegetable oil
1 tsp cumin seeds
10–12 fresh curry leaves

pressure cooker (optional)

SERVES 5

Drain the moong dhal, then transfer it to a pressure cooker with the salt, turmeric and boiling water. Close the pressure cooker and place over a medium heat. Cook for about 17 minutes or 7 whistles until the lentils have completely fallen apart. (If you don't have a pressure cooker, transfer the soaked and drained lentils to a large saucepan with 1 litre/quart of boiling water, the salt and turmeric. Cover with a lid and bring to the boil, then simmer over a medium heat for 30 minutes, topping up the water as needed.)

When the lentils are cooked, release the steam from the pressure cooker slowly (or remove the pan from the heat). Most of the water should have been absorbed during cooking, but gently whisk the lentils with any small amount that remains. Set aside.

Meanwhile, for the roasted cauliflower, preheat the oven to 180°C (350°F) Gas 4.

Pour the boiling water into a large saucepan and add the turmeric. Carefully tip in the cauliflower florets. Place over a medium heat and simmer for 3–4 minutes until starting to soften.

Drain the florets in a colander and leave to drip-dry while you prepare the seasoning. In a roasting pan, combine the vegetable oil, coarse sea salt, black pepper, cumin seeds, crushed coriander seeds, and the dried chilli flakes/hot red pepper flakes. Add the drained cauliflower and toss well to coat in the oil and spices. Roast the cauliflower in the preheated oven for 20 minutes or until soft in the middle and slightly charred on the outside.

Meanwhile, to finish the dhal, put the vegetable oil into a saucepan over a medium heat. Add the garlic and ginger pastes and fry for 1 minute until they lose their raw aroma and start to separate slightly. Add the chopped tomatoes and fry for 5–6 minutes until they soften and melt down.

Add the Kashmiri chilli/chili powder and ground turmeric and fry the spices in the tomato base for 2 minutes. Pour in the cooked moong dhal and mix well. Finally, stir in the garam masala and sea salt. Allow the dhal base to simmer over a gentle heat for 2–3 minutes.

Meanwhile, prepare the tadka. Put the oil into a small saucepan over a medium heat. Add the cumin seeds and allow them to sizzle in the hot oil for 30 seconds. Add the curry leaves and fry for 20 seconds, gently shaking the pan. Carefully pour the hot tadka oil over the dhal and mix in well.

Serve the dhal in bowls topped with the spiced roasted cauliflower florets.

MOONG DHAL WITH CRISPY LOTUS CHIPS

A recipe that celebrates the humble lotus root… a vegetable that spends its whole life hidden in muddy swamps while the lotus flower above basks in sunlight. Well, now it is the turn of the root to shine! Lotus roots are versatile and great at soaking up flavour. They turn golden and crunchy when shallow-fried, so together with this yellow dhal, the dish is as golden as an Indian summer sunset.

MOONG DHAL BASE

150 g/5½ oz. yellow split moong dhal, picked and rinsed, then soaked in 1 litre/quart lukewarm water for 2 hours
½ tsp fine sea salt
½ tsp ground turmeric
1 litre/quart boiling water

TO FINISH

3 tbsp vegetable oil
2 cardamom pods
3 cloves
2.5-cm/1-inch piece of cinnamon stick
½ tsp cumin seeds
1 onion, finely diced
½ tsp fine sea salt
1 tsp ginger paste
1 tsp garlic paste
½ tsp ground turmeric
½ tsp Kashmiri chilli/chili powder
50 ml/3½ tbsp boiling water (optional)
3 medium tomatoes, chopped
1 tsp palm sugar/jaggery
1 tsp garam masala

CRISPY LOTUS CHIPS

2 tbsp mustard seed oil
400 g/14 oz. can lotus roots, drained and thinly sliced into 5-mm/¼-inch thick slices
1 tsp chaat masala

pressure cooker (optional)

SERVES 5

Drain the moong dhal, then transfer it to a pressure cooker with the salt, turmeric and boiling water. Close the pressure cooker and place over a medium heat. Cook for about 17 minutes or 7 whistles until the lentils have completely fallen apart. (If you don't have a pressure cooker, transfer the soaked and drained lentils to a large saucepan with 1 litre/quart of boiling water, the salt and turmeric. Cover with a lid and bring to the boil, then simmer over a medium heat for 30 minutes, topping up with more boiling water as needed.)

When the lentils are cooked, release the steam from the pressure cooker slowly (or remove the pan from the heat). Most of the water should have been absorbed during cooking, but gently whisk the lentils with any small amount that remains. Set aside.

To finish the dhal, put the vegetable oil into a large saucepan over a medium heat. Add the cardamom pods, cloves and cinnamon stick and let them sizzle for 30 seconds to release their aromas into the hot oil. Sprinkle in the cumin seeds and let them sizzle for 30 seconds. Add the finely diced onion and salt and fry for 10–12 minutes until the onion has become buttery soft and golden brown – this will create a caramelized flavour which will carry throughout the dish.

Add the ginger and garlic pastes and fry for 1 minute. Add the ground turmeric and Kashmiri chilli/chili powder and fry for 30–60 seconds, stirring to coat the onion in the spices. If the pan gets too dry, add the boiling water and mix well to loosen the ingredients in the pan. Add the chopped tomatoes and palm sugar/jaggery and mix well. Cover the saucepan with a lid, turn the heat down to low and allow the tomatoes to collapse and melt down for 10 minutes, stirring frequently.

Meanwhile, prepare the crispy lotus chips for garnish. Heat the mustard seed oil in a non-stick frying pan/skillet and add the sliced lotus roots. Carefully shallow-fry in the hot oil for 5 minutes, turning over halfway through.

Turn off the heat, but leave the lotus roots in the pan. Sprinkle the chaat masala over the crispy lotus chips and gently toss in the pan for an even coverage. Set aside.

Returning to the dhal, add the cooked moong dhal and garam masala to the tomato and onion base and mix well. Simmer together for a final 2–3 minutes.

Divide the dhal between serving bowls and top with the crispy lotus chips.

YOGURTY MOONG DHAL

A dhal with a twist. These softened pearls of emerald-green moong dhal are steeped in a rich, thick, spiced yogurt sauce packed full of flavour and fresh heat.

MOONG DHAL BASE

100 g/3½ oz. whole green moong dhal, picked and rinsed, then soaked in 1 litre/quart lukewarm water overnight
1 litre/quart boiling water
1 tsp fine sea salt, plus extra to taste

YOGURT SAUCE

320 g/1½ cups natural/plain yogurt
1 tbsp chickpea/gram flour
1 tsp fine sea salt
½ tsp ground turmeric
1 tsp Holy Trinity Paste (see page 13)
1 tsp palm sugar/jaggery

TADKA

3 tbsp ghee (or butter)
3 cloves
1 tsp cumin seeds
1 garlic clove, grated
½ tsp dried chilli flakes/hot red pepper flakes
10–15 fresh curry leaves

TO FINISH

5–6 fresh coriander/cilantro stems, roughly chopped
warm Roti Breads, to serve (see page 89)

pressure cooker (optional)

SERVES 4

Drain the moong dhal, then transfer it to a pressure cooker with the boiling water and salt. Close the pressure cooker and place over a medium heat. Cook for about 20 minutes or 5–6 whistles until the lentils are soft but still retain their shape. (If you don't have a pressure cooker, you can cook the soaked and drained lentils in a large saucepan with 1 litre/quart of boiling water and the salt. Cover with a lid and bring to the boil, then simmer over a medium heat for 30 minutes, topping up the boiling water as needed.)

When the lentils are cooked, release the steam from the pressure cooker slowly (or remove the pan from the heat). Most of the water should have been absorbed during cooking, but gently crush the lentils with any small amount that remains. Set aside.

For the yogurt sauce, combine the yogurt, chickpea/gram flour, salt, turmeric and holy trinity paste in a medium saucepan. Whisk together well to remove any lumps, then pour in 200 ml/generous 3/4 cup of cold water and whisk again. Place the pan over a low-medium heat and bring to a gentle simmer for 3–4 minutes, whisking constantly to prevent the yogurt from splitting.

Add the cooked and drained moong dhal and the palm sugar/jaggery and mix in well. Allow the mixture to simmer gently for 2–3 minutes, stirring occasionally.

Meanwhile, for the tadka, put the ghee (or butter) into a small saucepan over a medium heat. Add the cloves and cumin seeds and fry for 30 seconds until they crackle in the hot oil. Add the garlic, dried chilli flakes/hot red pepper flakes and curry leaves and fry for 10 seconds. Pour the tadka oil into the dhal and stir well. To finish, stir in the chopped coriander/cilantro and adjust the seasoning.

Serve with warm roti breads.

MOONG DHAL CREPES WITH SAMBHAR DHAL

These gluten-free crêpes, traditionally known as dosas, are a national treasure in the south of India. Made from ground soaked moong dhal, the dosa batter is spiced with asafoetida powder, which gives them a pungent flavour. This recipe showcases the versatility of the humble lentil, which is able to create a crispy-textured crêpe as well as the accompanying sambhar – a spiced and flavoursome toor dhal soup finished with tamarind and boasting a selection of vegetables.

MOONG DHAL CRÊPES

350 g/12 oz. yellow split moong dhal
1 litre/quart lukewarm water
1 tsp fine sea salt
pinch of asafoetida powder
vegetable oil, for shallow-frying

SAMBHAR MASALA

1 tbsp coriander seeds
1 tbsp cumin seeds
1 tbsp mustard seeds
1 tbsp whole black peppercorns
1 tbsp split channa dhal, picked
1 tbsp split white urad dhal, picked
20 fresh curry leaves
2 dried long red chillies/chiles
½ tsp asafoetida powder
½ tsp ground turmeric

SAMBHAR DHAL

125 g/4½ oz. toor dhal
500 ml/2 cups plus 2 tbsp boiling water
½ tsp fine sea salt
½ tsp ground turmeric

SAMBHAR VEGETABLES

4 tbsp vegetable oil
1 onion, finely chopped
pinch of fine sea salt
30 g/1 oz. piece of fresh ginger, peeled and grated
1 tsp Sambhar Masala (see left)
50 ml/3½ tbsp boiling water (optional)
1 carrot, peeled and chopped into 2.5-cm/1-inch chunks
2 medium tomatoes, roughly chopped
1 aubergine/eggplant chopped into 2.5-cm/ 1-inch chunks
100 g/3½ oz. green beans, topped and tailed and halved
200 ml/generous ¾ cup boiling water

TO FINISH

½ tbsp tamarind paste
2 tsp palm sugar/ jaggery
5–6 fresh coriander/ cilantro stems, roughly chopped

TADKA

3 tbsp vegetable oil
1 tsp cumin seeds
1 tsp mustard seeds
1 green chilli/chile, slit in half lengthways
10–12 fresh curry leaves
pinch of asafoetida powder

pressure cooker (optional)

SERVES 4

Carefully pick through the moong dhal to remove any stones. Placc it in a colander and rinse well under cold running water until the water runs clear. Leave the moong dhal to soak for 3 hours in the lukewarm water – after the dhal has been soaking for about 1½ hours, start to prepare the sambhar masala for the sambhar dhal.

Place a dry frying pan/skillet over a high heat and add the coriander seeds, cumin seeds, mustard seeds, whole peppercorns, channa dhal and white urad dhal. Toast the blend of spices and dhals for 2–3 minutes, until the spices release their aromas, shaking the pan constantly so that the spices don't burn. Add the curry leaves, dried chillies/ chiles, asafoetida powder and ground turmeric and toast for a further 30 seconds. Transfer the mixture to a spice or coffee grinder and blitz until you are left with a coarse powder. If you don't have a spice or coffee grinder, you can do it the traditional way with a pestle and mortar. Set aside until required.

For the sambhar dhal, pick through the toor dhal to remove any stones. Place it in a colander and rinse under cold running water until the water runs clear. Transfer to a pressure cooker with the boiling water, the salt and turmeric. Close the pressure cooker and place over a medium heat. Cook for about 10 minutes or 6–7 whistles. (If you don't have a pressure cooker, you can cook the lentils in a large saucepan with 1 litre/quart of boiling water, the salt and turmeric. Cover with a lid and bring to the boil, then simmer over a medium heat for 60–70 minutes, topping up with more boiling water as needed.)

While the toor dhal is cooking, prepare the sambhar vegetables. Put the vegetable oil into another large saucepan over a medium heat. Add the onion and salt and fry for 7–8 minutes until soft and golden.

Add the grated ginger and fry for 1 further minute. Add the 1 teaspoon of sambhar masala spice blend and mix to coat the onion in the spices. Fry the masala for 1 further minute. If the pan starts to dry out, add the boiling water to loosen the ingredients.

Add the diced carrot, mix well and fry for 5 minutes. Tip in the chunks of tomato, cover the pan with a lid and fry for 5 minutes until the tomatoes have started to soften and melt down to make the sauce base.

Meanwhile, when the lentils are cooked and completely soft, release the steam from the pressure cooker slowly (or remove the pan from the heat). Most of the water should have been absorbed during cooking, but gently crush the lentils with any small amount that does remain.

Add the chunks of aubergine/eggplant to the sambhar vegetable mixture, then pour in the cooked toor dhal and stir well. Simmer for 5 minutes, then add the green beans along with the boiling water. Again, mix the contents of the pan, then turn the heat down to low and simmer the sambhar dhal mixture for 12–15 minutes until all of the vegetables have softened, then remove from the heat.

Meanwhile, prepare the batter for the moong dhal crêpes. By now, the moong dhal should have had a full 3 hours of soaking.

Drain the lentils but reserve the soaking water. In a bowl, mix the lentils with the salt and asafoetida powder. In small batches, place some of the lentils in a wet grinder, if you have one (or use a coffee or herb grinder or a powerful food processor). Process the lentils down, adding 2–3 tablespoons of the reserved soaking water per batch, until the paste turns into a thick batter. Transfer the ground lentil batter to a large mixing bowl as you work. The batter should be smooth with some coarse bits of lentils remaining and of a pouring consistency, similar to an American pancake batter. Cover the bowl with clingfilm/plastic wrap and set aside to rest at room temperature while you complete the sambhar vegetables.

Add the tamarind paste to the sambhar dhal, followed by the palm sugar/jaggery and the chopped coriander/cilantro. Stir well and simmer gently for 2–3 minutes while you prepare the tadka.

Put the vegetable oil in a small saucepan over a medium heat. Add the cumin and mustard seeds and fry in the hot oil for 1 minute or until they crackle. Then throw in the slit green chillie/chile, curry leaves and asafoetida powder. Give the pan a good shake and then tip the entire contents into the sambhar dhal. Stir well and remove the pan from the heat. Cover the sambhar dhal with a lid and set aside to rest until ready to serve with the moong dhal crêpes.

Give the crêpe batter a good whisk. Place a medium-sized frying pan/skillet (I use an 18-cm/7-inch one) over a medium heat and pour in a tablespoon of vegetable oil. Tilt the pan to evenly coat the base in the oil. Ensure the oil is hot, then reduce the heat to low-medium. Scoop up a ladleful of the batter and pour into the pan. Working quickly, use the base of the ladle to spread the batter out in the hot oil in circular motions. Once spread out, the batter will cook very quickly (in 1–2 minutes). As soon as it has browned on one side, carefully flip the crêpe over and fry on the other side for 1–2 minutes. Remove from the pan to a warm plate. Continue to fry the rest of the batter in the same way, stacking the moong dhal crêpes on the warmed plate as you finish.

When all the crêpes are ready, place the saucepan of sambhar dhal back over a medium heat and bring back up to a simmer for a few minutes until warmed through.

Serve the moong dhal crêpes with generous bowls of the sambhar dhal soup for dipping into.

RAJMA DHAL

Rajma dhal also goes by the name of red kidney beans, which are widely available cooked and canned or raw and dried. Rajma are an integral part of North Indian cuisine because they're such a popular choice for vegetarians. When cooked, the beans retain their shape, which is satisfying to bite into, with creamy-textured flesh inside. They are low in fat, rich in complex carbohydrates, protein, vitamins and minerals. Rajma Dhal (see page 80) is the most famous dish, followed by Rajma Makhani (see page 84), which when finished off with butter and cream, makes a rich and luxurious dish fit for the Mughals of India. Nevertheless, red kidney beans are also a popular and inexpensive staple bean for many people across the globe, especially in North and South America.

SPINACH RAJMA DHAL

Rich in iron, versatile spinach is not only tasty but also highly nutritious. In this dish, the rajma (red kidney beans) are cooked until soft, smooth and creamy, then immersed in a sweet and aromatic spiced tomato sauce. The spinach is blended to create a buttery-soft purée, which when added, transforms the tomato sauce into a creamy emerald-green sea, studded with the ruby-red kidney beans.

RAJMA DHAL BASE

200 g/7 oz. rajma dhal, picked and rinsed, then soaked in 1 litre/quart boiling water overnight

1.5 litres/quarts boiling water

RAJMA MASALA

4 tbsp vegetable oil

1 tsp cumin seeds

1 onion, roughly chopped

½ tsp fine sea salt

1 tsp ginger paste

1 tsp garlic paste

½ tsp ground turmeric

½ tsp ground cumin

½ tsp ground coriander

½ tsp Kashmiri chilli/chili powder

50 ml/3½ tbsp boiling water (optional)

1 tbsp tomato purée/paste

3 large tomatoes, cores and seeds removed, roughly chopped

1 tsp palm sugar/jaggery

½ tsp garam masala

1 tbsp freshly chopped coriander/cilantro

Naan Breads (see page 108) or pilau rice, to serve (optional)

SPINACH PURÉE

2 tbsp mustard seed oil

200 g/7 oz. fresh baby spinach

pinch of fine sea salt

pressure cooker (optional)

SERVES 4

Drain the soaked rajma dhal, discarding the soaking water. Transfer the soaked dhal to the pressure cooker with the fresh boiling water. Close the pressure cooker and place over a medium heat. Cook for about 20 minutes or 5 whistles, or until the beans have softened but still retain their shape. (If you don't have a pressure cooker, place the soaked and drained beans in a large saucepan with 1.5 litres/quarts of fresh boiling water. Cover with a lid and boil for 10 minutes to kill off any toxins, then simmer for 60–70 minutes over a low heat, topping up with more boiling water as needed.)

While the beans are cooking, begin to make the rajma masala sauce. Put the vegetable oil into a large saucepan over a medium heat. Add the cumin seeds and let them sizzle in the hot oil for 1 minute. Add the onion and the salt and fry for 10 minutes until the onion is soft and golden brown.

Add the ginger and garlic pastes and fry for 1 minute until the raw aroma has gone and the pastes are starting to separate. Add the ground turmeric, cumin, coriander and Kashmiri chilli/chili powder, stir to coat the onion in the spices and fry for a further 1–2 minutes. Add the boiling water to loosen the ingredients if the pan gets too dry.

Add the tomato purée/paste, mix well and fry for 2 minutes. Add the chopped tomatoes and palm sugar/jaggery and mix well. Cover the saucepan with a lid, turn the heat down to low and let the tomatoes soften and melt down for 10 minutes, stirring frequently.

Meanwhile, prepare the spinach purée. Put the mustard seed oil in a frying pan/skillet over a medium heat. Add the baby spinach and salt and gently fry for about 2 minutes until completely wilted. Transfer the wilted spinach to a small food processor or even a pestle and mortar and blend or crush to a smooth paste. If the spinach purée is too thick or difficult to blend, add 1–2 tablespoons of water to help achieve a smooth consistency. Set aside.

When the rajma dhal is cooked, release the steam from the pressure cooker slowly (or remove the pan from the heat). Drain off any excess water, then add the beans to the sauce base along with the boiling water. Mix well and simmer for 10–12 minutes. Add the spinach purée and garam masala. Stir well and check the seasoning. The consistency of this rajma dhal should be thick and stew-like.

Serve in bowls, garnished with the chopped coriander/cilantro. Enjoy with warm naan breads or pilau rice, if you like.

RAJMA MUGHLAI DHAL

Dating back to the medieval period when the mughal emperors ruled India and Pakistan, this kidney bean curry is rich and creamy, yet light – fit for an emperor's feast!

RAJMA DHAL BASE

200 g/7 oz. rajma dhal, picked and rinsed, then soaked in 1 litre/quart boiling water overnight
1.5 litres/quarts boiling water

MUGHLAI SAUCE

3 tbsp vegetable oil
1 onion, finely chopped
1 tsp fine sea salt, plus
1 tbsp ginger paste
1 tbsp garlic paste
½ tsp ground turmeric
½ tsp ground cumin
½ tsp ground coriander
¼ tsp Kashmiri chilli/chili powder
50 ml/3½ tbsp boiling water (optional)
1 tsp tomato purée/paste
3 large tomatoes, chopped
1 tbsp caster/granulated sugar
125 ml/½ cup boiling water
115 ml/scant ½ cup double/heavy cream
2 tbsp ground almonds
2 tbsp sultanas/golden raisins
1 tbsp ghee (or butter)
1 tsp garam masala
Roti Breads (see page 89), to serve

pressure cooker (optional)

SERVES 4

Drain the soaked rajma dhal, discarding the soaking water. Transfer the soaked dhal to the pressure cooker with the fresh boiling water. Close the pressure cooker and place over a medium heat. Cook for about 20 minutes or 5 whistles or until the beans have softened but still retain their shape. (If you don't have a pressure cooker, drain and discard the soaking water, then place the beans in a large saucepan with 1.5 litres/quarts boiling water. Cover with a lid and boil for 10 minutes to kill off any toxins, then simmer for 60 minutes over a low heat, topping up with more boiling water as needed.)

Meanwhile, begin to make the mughlai sauce. Put the vegetable oil into a large saucepan over a medium heat. Add the onion and salt and fry for 10 minutes until soft and golden brown.

Add the ginger and garlic pastes and fry for 1 minute. Stir in the ground turmeric, cumin, coriander and Kashmiri chilli/chili powder and fry for 1–2 minutes, adding the boiling water to loosen the ingredients if the pan gets too dry. Add the tomato purée/paste, mix well and fry for 2 minutes. Add the chopped tomatoes and caster/granulated sugar and mix well. Cover the saucepan with a lid, turn the heat down to low and simmer for 10 minutes until the tomatoes have melted down, stirring frequently.

Meanwhile, when the kidney beans are cooked, release the steam from the pressure cooker slowly (or remove the pan from the heat). Drain off any excess water, then add the beans to the sauce base along with the boiling water. Mix well and simmer together for 10–12 minutes. Finally, stir in the cream, almonds, sultanas/golden raisins, ghee (or butter) and garam masala. Simmer for 2 minutes, then check and correct the seasoning before serving with roti breads.

RAJMA MAKHANI DHAL

Makhani dhal is to North India what carbonara is to the Italians – rich, comforting and indulgent. And this recipe oozes indulgence, from the soft beans to the silky tomato, cream and butter sauce. Not one for every day, but definitely one if you want to impress guests with a decadent meal! Despite the richness, this dish boasts much flavour from the earthy spices, fragrant tadka oil and the depth and smokiness of the dried fenugreek leaves.

RAJMA DHAL BASE

200 g/7 oz. rajma dhal, picked and rinsed, then soaked in 1 litre/quart boiling water overnight
1.5 litres/quarts boiling water

MAKHANI SAUCE

3 tbsp vegetable oil
1 onion, finely chopped
1 tsp fine sea salt, plus extra to taste
1 tbsp ginger paste
1 tbsp garlic paste
½ tsp ground turmeric
½ tsp ground cumin
½ tsp ground coriander
¼ tsp Kashmiri chilli/chili powder
1 tsp dried fenugreek leaves
50 ml/3½ tbsp boiling water (optional)
1 tsp tomato purée/paste
3 large tomatoes, chopped
1 tbsp runny honey
125 ml/½ cup boiling water
115 ml/scant ½ cup double/heavy cream
1 tbsp unsalted butter
1 tsp garam masala
Roti Breads (see page 89), to serve

TADKA

2 tbsp ghee (or butter)
2 cloves
2 cardamom pods
½ tsp cumin seeds

pressure cooker (optional)

SERVES 4

Drain the soaked rajma dhal, discarding the soaking water. Transfer the soaked dhal to the pressure cooker with the fresh boiling water. Close the pressure cooker and place over a medium heat. Cook for about 20 minutes or 5 whistles or until the beans have softened but still retain their shape. (If you don't have a pressure cooker, drain and discard the soaking water, then place the beans in a large saucepan with 1.5 litres/quarts of fresh boiling water. Cover with a lid and boil for 10 minutes to kill off any toxins, then simmer for 60 minutes over a low heat, topping up with more boiling water as needed.)

While the red kidney beans are cooking, begin to make the makhani sauce. Put the vegetable oil into a large saucepan over a medium heat and add the onion and salt. Fry the onion for about 10 minutes until soft and golden brown.

Add the ginger and garlic pastes and fry for 1 minute until they begin to separate and the raw aroma has cooked off. Add the ground turmeric, cumin, coriander, Kashmiri chilli/chili powder and dried fenugreek leaves. Stir to coat the onion in the spices and fry for a further 1–2 minutes. Add the boiling water to loosen the ingredients if the pan gets too dry. Add the tomato purée/paste, mix well and fry for 2 minutes. Add the chopped tomatoes and honey and mix well. Cover the saucepan with a lid, then turn the heat down to low and allow the base to simmer and the tomatoes to melt down for 10 minutes, stirring frequently.

Meanwhile, when the kidney beans are cooked, release the steam from the pressure cooker slowly (or remove the pan from the heat). Drain off any excess water, then add the beans to the sauce base along with the boiling water. Mix well and simmer gently for 10–12 minutes, then add the cream, butter and garam masala and stir in with the rest of the ingredients. Simmer gently for 2–3 minutes while you prepare the tadka.

Put the ghee (or butter) into a small saucepan over a medium heat and add the cloves, cardamom pods and cumin seeds. Fry the spices for 30 seconds until the cumin seeds crackle. Gently pour the hot tadka, along with all of the spices, into the simmering rajma makhani dhal and stir well to combine. Simmer for 1 final minute.

Check and correct the seasoning before serving. This indulgent dish goes perfectly with warm moreish roti breads, if you like.

RAJMA DHAL WITH SPICED SQUASH, CUCUMBER RAITA AND ROTI BREADS

This flavoursome kidney bean dhal is crowned with roasted spiced butternut squash. It's served with a cooling cucumber raita and roti breads, both of which are delicious with many other dishes, too.

RAJMA DHAL BASE

250 g/9 oz. rajma dhal, picked and rinsed, then soaked in 1 litre/ quart boiling water overnight
1.5 litres/quarts boiling water

SAUCE

4 tbsp vegetable oil
1 onion, finely chopped
pinch of fine sea salt
1 tsp ginger paste
1 tsp garlic paste
½ tsp ground turmeric
½ tsp ground cumin
½ tsp ground coriander
½ tsp Kashmiri chilli/ chili powder
50 ml/3½ tbsp boiling water (optional)
1 tbsp tomato purée/paste
3 large tomatoes, cores and seeds removed, roughly chopped
100 ml/⅓ cup plus 1 tbsp boiling water
1 tsp palm sugar/ jaggery
½ tsp garam masala
1 tbsp freshly chopped coriander/cilantro

TADKA

4 tbsp vegetable oil
3 cloves
½ tsp cumin seeds
½ tsp mustard seeds
½ tsp peeled and grated fresh ginger
20 fresh curry leaves

SPICED SQUASH

½ butternut, peeled and chopped into 2.5-cm/1-inch chunks
3 tbsp vegetable oil
1 tsp cumin seeds
1 tsp crushed coriander seeds
½ tsp fine sea salt
½ tsp crushed dried chilli flakes/hot red pepper flakes

TO SERVE

Cucumber Raita **(see page 89)**
Roti Breads **(see page 89)**

roasting pan, lined with baking parchment

pressure cooker (optional)

SERVES 4

Preheat the oven to 180°C (350°F) Gas 4.

In a mixing bowl, combine all of the ingredients for the dhana jeeru butternut squash and mix well to ensure the chunks of squash are well coated. Spread the spiced squash evenly over the lined roasting pan. Roast in the preheated oven for 30 minutes, turning halfway through, until softened and slightly charred. Keep warm until required.

Drain the soaked rajma dhal, discarding the soaking water. Transfer the soaked dhal to the pressure cooker with the fresh boiling water. Close the pressure cooker and place over a medium heat. Cook for about 20 minutes or 5 whistles or until the beans have softened but still retain their shape. (If you don't have a pressure cooker, drain and discard the soaking water, then place the beans in a large saucepan with 1.5 litres/quarts of fresh boiling water. Cover with a lid and boil for 10 minutes to kill off any toxins, then simmer for 60 minutes over a low heat, topping up with more water as needed.)

While the beans are cooking, begin to make the sauce. Put the vegetable oil into a large saucepan over a medium heat. Add the onion and salt and fry for about 10 minutes until soft and golden brown.

Add the ginger and garlic pastes and fry for 1 minute until the raw aroma has gone. Add the ground turmeric, cumin, coriander and Kashmiri chilli/chili powder and stir to coat the onion in the spices. Add the boiling water to loosen the ingredients if the pan gets too dry. Add the tomato purée/paste, mix well and fry for 1 minute. Add the chopped tomatoes, then cover with a lid and turn the heat to low. Let the tomatoes melt and soften for 10 minutes, stirring regularly.

By now, the beans should be cooked through. Release the steam from the pressure cooker slowly (or remove the pan from the heat). Drain off any excess water, then add the beans to the sauce base along with the boiling water. Mix well and simmer gently for 10–12 minutes. Add the palm sugar/jaggery, garam masala and chopped coriander/cilantro and stir. Simmer gently for 3 minutes while you prepare the tadka.

Put the vegetable oil into a small saucepan. Add the cloves, then after 10 seconds, add the cumin seeds and mustard seeds and let them sizzle for 1 minute. Add the grated ginger and curry leaves and gently shake the pan. Carefully tip the hot tadka oil and all the spices into the rajma dhal and mix well. Simmer together for 1 final minute.

Ladle the rajma dhal into serving bowls and top with the warm roasted dhana jeeru butternut squash. Serve with cucumber raita and roti breads.

ROTI BREADS

300 g/2 cups medium chapatti/fine ground whole-wheat flour
2 tbsp vegetable oil
225 ml/scant 1 cup boiling water
plain/all-purpose flour, for dusting
melted butter, for brushing

MAKES 12

Combine the chapatti/fine ground whole-wheat flour and oil in a mixing bowl and mix well so that the flour grains are enrobed in the oil. Carefully add the boiling water and gradually mix with a fork so that the mixture starts to come together as a dough. Knead the dough for 5–6 minutes until soft and smooth.

Divide the dough into 12 equal pieces. Roll each piece into a ball and smooth out any cracks, then flatten each one slightly between your palms so that you have 12 round discs with thicker centres.

Lightly dust a work surface with a little plain/all-purpose flour, then dredge the discs of dough in the flour on both sides. Roll each floured disc out to a circumference of about 15 cm/6 inches.

Set a heavy-based frying pan/skillet over a medium heat. Place one dough disc into the hot pan and heat for 15–20 seconds. Flip over and cook on the other side – you will see that brown circular marks have appeared underneath. Flip again to complete the cooking on the half-cooked side. As it cooks you will see small air pockets begin to form. Use a clean kitchen cloth, neatly scrunched up into a ball, to gently press on the air pockets for about 12 seconds to encourage the air to distribute evenly and form one big air pocket.

Remove the roti bread from the pan to a clean, warm plate and brush the top with a little melted butter. Repeat the cooking process with the next dough disc and stack the cooked breads one on top of the other, until all of the breads are cooked.

As each bread is cooked, stack them on top of each other on a plate to stop them from drying out. Serve immediately or wrap the breads tightly in clingfilm/plastic wrap and freeze for up to 1 month.

CUCUMBER RAITA

5–6 fresh mint sprigs, leaves picked and stems discarded, plus extra to garnish
½ cucumber
250 g/scant 1¼ cups natural/plain yogurt
sea salt, to taste

SERVES 4

Finely chop the mint leaves and grate the cucumber. Mix all the ingredients together in a small bowl, adding salt to taste. Garnish with extra mint leaves, if you like.

ALOO RAJMA DHAL

This delightful dish, typical of North Indian cuisine, is testament to the delicious and substantial things that can be eaten on a vegan diet! Raw potatoes are simmered in a spiced broth until soft, soaking up the aromatic flavour of the spices as they tenderize. The broth is then developed with meaty tomatoes, which melt into the broth to form a sauce. The silky ruby-red kidney beans are added and simmered with garam masala and coriander/cilantro for a final aromatic boost.

RAJMA DHAL BASE

200 g/7 oz. rajma dhal, picked and rinsed, then soaked in 1 litre/quart boiling water overnight

1.5 litres/quarts boiling water

ALOO SAUCE

4 tbsp vegetable oil

3 cloves

½ tsp cumin seeds

½ tsp mustard seeds

1 onion, roughly chopped

½ tsp fine sea salt

1 tsp ginger paste

1 tsp garlic paste

½ tsp ground turmeric

½ tsp ground cumin

½ tsp ground coriander

½ tsp Kashmiri chilli/chili powder

50 ml/3½ tbsp boiling water (optional)

2 Maris Piper potatoes (peeled and chopped into 1-cm/½-inch chunks, soaked in cold water until needed

500 ml/2 cups plus 2 tbsp boiling water

3 large tomatoes, cores and seeds removed, roughly chopped

1 tsp palm sugar/jaggery

½ tsp garam masala

1 tbsp freshly chopped coriander/cilantro

pressure cooker (optional)

SERVES 4

Drain the soaked rajma dhal, discarding the soaking water. Transfer the soaked dhal to the pressure cooker with the fresh boiling water. Close the pressure cooker and place over a medium heat. Cook for about 20 minutes or 5 whistles or until the beans have softened but still retain their shape. (If you don't have a pressure cooker, drain and discard the soaking water, then place the beans in a large saucepan with 1.5 litres/quarts of fresh boiling water. Cover with a lid and boil for 10 minutes to kill off any toxins, then simmer for 60 minutes over a low heat, topping up the boiling water as needed.)

While the beans are cooking, begin to make the aloo sauce. Put the oil into a large saucepan over a medium heat. Add the cloves and fry for 20 seconds in the hot oil. Add the cumin and mustard seeds and allow them to sizzle in the hot oil for 1 minute. Add the chopped onion and salt and fry for about 10 minutes until the onion is soft and golden.

Add the ginger and garlic pastes and fry for 1 minute until the raw aroma has gone and they are beginning to separate. Add the ground turmeric, cumin, coriander and Kashmiri chilli/chili powder. Stir to coat the onion in the spices and fry for a further 1–2 minutes. Add the boiling water to loosen the ingredients if the pan gets too dry. Drain the peeled and chopped potatoes and add to the onion along with the boiling water. Boil the potatoes in the spiced broth for 10 minutes until just softened.

Add the chopped tomatoes and palm sugar/jaggery and mix well. Simmer for a further 10 minutes until the tomatoes have softened and melted and the sauce has thickened, stirring gently from time to time.

By now, the beans should be cooked through. Release the steam from the pressure cooker slowly (or remove the pan from the heat). Drain off any excess water, then add the beans to the sauce base and mix well. Let the aloo rajma simmer gently with the tomatoes and potatoes for a further 2 minutes.

Sprinkle in the garam masala and chopped coriander/cilantro and mix well before dividing into serving bowls.

LAL CHORI DHAL

More commonly known as aduki beans, chori is a legume that is thousands of years old. It is grown all over East Asia and in the mountainous Himalayan province. In Southeast Asia, the ingredient is used as the base of the popular red bean paste, which is combined with sugar and used to make many desserts. In India, savoury lal (red) chori dhal is revered all over the country, most likely because of its extensive list of nutritious benefits – it is rich in fibre and protein and great for digestion, all of which are in keeping with a health-giving ayurvedic lifestyle. Lal chori dhal has a neutral but slightly nutty flavour, which makes it a great central ingredient for adding other flavours to. Being a bean, however, it can take a little longer to cook than other lentils.

LAL CHORI DHAL AND PANEER SALAD

A strong competitor in the battle of summery salads, this dish is my version of a Mediterranean Greek salad. Ok, so the feta cheese has been replaced with charred paneer and there are no black olives, but this dish still hits the same refreshing and satisfying notes. Here, the flavour of the humble lal chori dhal (aduki bean) stands proud, and combines beautifully with red onion, cucumber, (bell) peppers and a zingy mustard seed oil, lemon juice and mint dressing.

LAL CHORI DHAL BASE

200 g/7 oz. lal chori dhal, picked and rinsed, then soaked in 1 litre/quart lukewarm water overnight
1.5 litres/quarts boiling water
1 tsp fine sea salt

TOSSED SALAD

½ tsp cumin seeds
½ tsp coriander seeds
freshly squeezed juice of ½ lemon
2 tbsp mustard seed oil
½ tsp fine sea salt
1 red onion, finely chopped
½ cucumber, roughly chopped
1 red (bell) pepper, deseeded and finely chopped
1 green (bell) pepper, deseeded and finely chopped
5–7 fresh mint sprigs, leaves picked and roughly chopped

Cucumber Raita, to serve (see page 89)

CHARRED PANEER

4 tbsp vegetable oil
½ tsp fine sea salt
½ tsp Kashmiri chilli/chili powder
freshly squeezed juice of ½ lemon
250 g/9 oz. paneer, diced

pressure cooker (optional)

SERVES 6

Drain the soaked chori dhal, discarding the soaking water, and transfer to a pressure cooker with the boiling water and salt. Close the pressure cooker and place over a medium heat. Cook for about 25 minutes or 6 whistles. (If you don't have a pressure cooker, you can cook the soaked and drained chori dhal in a large saucepan with 1.5 litres/quarts of boiling water and the salt. Cover with a lid and bring to the boil, then simmer over a medium heat for 60–70 minutes, topping up with more boiling water as needed.)

When the lal chori dhal is cooked, release the steam from the pressure cooker slowly (or remove the pan from the heat). Drain the chori dhal in a sieve/strainer and rinse under cold running water for a few seconds. Drain well again and set aside.

For the salad, put a large frying pan/skillet over a medium heat and add the cumin and coriander seeds. Toast together for 30 seconds, shaking the pan. Transfer to a pestle and mortar and crush the seeds coarsely. Keep the pan out as you will use it again to char the paneer.

Place the crushed toasted seeds in a mixing bowl and add the lemon juice, mustard seed oil, salt and chopped red onion. Mix well to coat the onion in the dressing and set aside for the onion to soften while you prepare the rest of the salad.

For the charred paneer, stir together 2 tablespoons of the vegetable oil, the salt, Kashmiri chilli/chili powder and the lemon juice in a mixing bowl. Tip in the diced paneer and toss to coat in the marinade.

Put the remaining 2 tablespoons of vegetable oil into the frying pan/skillet you used to toast the spices and place over a medium heat. Add the marinated paneer and fry for 5–6 minutes, turning regularly, until all the chunks are golden brown all over. Transfer to a plate lined with paper towels to drain off any excess oil.

To the bowl of dressed onion, add the cooked and cooked lal chori dhal, the chopped cucumber, the chopped red and green (bell) peppers and the chopped mint leaves. Toss well to ensure all of the ingredients are coated in the dressing. Add the fried chunks of paneer and toss gently before serving in individual bowls.

Being a summery dish, serving this with a dollop of cooling cucumber raita adds a lovely freshness.

CHORI DIP WITH BANG BANG CAULI

Here, tender lal chori dhal are puréed to form a richly spiced wholesome dip, similar in texture to hummus. Bang bang cauliflower makes perfect crudités for dipping.

LAL CHORI DHAL DIP

100 g/3½ oz. lal chori dhal, picked and rinsed then soaked in 500 ml/ 2 cups plus 2 tbsp lukewarm water overnight
1.5 litres/quarts boiling water
½ tsp fine sea salt
fresh juice of 1 lemon
5–6 fresh coriander/ cilantro stems, roughly chopped
3 tbsp vegetable oil

BANG BANG CAULIFLOWER

1 litre/quart boiling water
1 tsp ground turmeric
1 whole cauliflower, cut into florets
3 tbsp vegetable oil
½ tsp coarse sea salt
½ tsp black pepper
½ tsp cumin seeds
½ tsp crushed coriander seeds
½ tsp dried chilli flakes/ hot red pepper flakes
20–25 fresh curry leaves

TADKA

4 tbsp vegetable oil
½ tsp mustard seeds
½ tsp ginger paste
1 tbsp desiccated/dried shredded coconut

pressure cooker (optional)

SERVES 4

Drain the lal chori dhal, discarding the soaking water, and transfer to a pressure cooker with the boiling water and the salt. Close the pressure cooker, place over a medium heat and cook for about 40 minutes or 12 whistles until the beans are falling apart. (If you don't have a pressure cooker, cook the soaked and drained dhal in a saucepan with 1 litre/quart of boiling water and the salt. Cover with a lid and bring to the boil, then simmer over a medium heat for 50–60 minutes, topping up the water as needed.)

While the dhal is cooking, prepare the cauliflower. Preheat the oven to 180°C (350°F) Gas 4. Put the boiling water and turmeric into a large saucepan over a medium heat. Add the cauliflower and simmer for 3–4 minutes until just softened. Drain and set aside.

In a roasting pan, combine the vegetable oil, coarse sea salt, black pepper, cumin seeds, crushed coriander seeds, chilli flakes/hot red pepper flakes and fresh curry leaves. Add the blanched cauliflower and toss well in the oil and spices. Roast in the preheated oven for 20 minutes or until the cauliflower is charred on the outside.

When the lal chori dhal is cooked, release the steam from the pressure cooker slowly (or remove the pan from the heat). Drain the chori, place it in a food processor and blend to a purée. Leave it chunky (how I like mine) or blend for longer and add some water if you prefer it smooth. Transfer the chori dip to a mixing bowl and mix in the salt, lemon juice and coriander/cilantro and oil. Set aside.

For the tadka, put the vegetable oil into a saucepan over a medium heat. Add the mustard seeds and fry for 30 seconds. Add the ginger paste and coconut and stir into the hot oil for 30 seconds. Pour the oil into the lal chori dhal dip and mix well. Remove the roasted cauliflower from the oven and serve with the chori dhal dip.

COCONUT AND ROASTED BEETROOT LAL CHORI DHAL

Traditionally used in South Indian cuisine, coconut milk adds rich yet light indulgence to this dish. The softened pearls of lal chori dhal are simmered in the fragrantly spiced coconut milk sauce, with smoky mustard seeds to balance out the sweetness. Transforming the spiced chori from a curry to a satisfying stew-like meal however, is the addition of the earthy roasted beetroot/beet chunks.

LAL CHORI DHAL BASE

200 g/7 oz. lal chori dhal, picked and rinsed, then soaked in 1 litre/quart lukewarm water overnight
1.25 litres/quarts boiling water
1 tsp fine sea salt

MASALA SAUCE

3 tbsp vegetable oil
3 cloves
2 cardamom pods
2.5-cm/1-inch piece of cinnamon stick
1 tsp cumin seeds
1 tsp mustard seeds
1 onion, finely chopped
½ tsp fine sea salt
1 tsp garlic purée
1 tsp ginger purée
½ tsp ground turmeric
½ tsp ground cumin
½ tsp ground coriander
½ tsp Kashmiri chilli/chili powder
4 tomatoes, roughly chopped
1 tsp palm sugar/jaggery
125 ml/½ cup coconut milk
1 tsp garam masala
5–7 fresh coriander/cilantro stems, roughly chopped
Roti Breads (see page 89), to serve

ROASTED BEETROOT

2 raw beetroot/beet, peeled and chopped into 2.5-cm/1-inch chunks (roughly 500 g/3 cups)
2 tbsp vegetable oil
½ tsp fine sea salt
½ tsp freshly ground black pepper

pressure cooker (optional)

SERVES 4–5

Preheat the oven to 180°C (350°F) Gas 4.

Place the chopped chunks of beetroot/ beet in a roasting pan, drizzle over the vegetable oil and sprinkle over the salt and black pepper. Roast in the preheated oven for 40 minutes or until softened, turning halfway through.

Meanwhile, drain the soaked lal chori dhal discarding the soaking water, and transfer to a pressure cooker with the boiling water and salt. Close the pressure cooker and place over a medium heat. Cook for about 30 minutes or 8 whistles. (If you don't have a pressure cooker, you can cook the soaked and drained chori dhal in a large saucepan with 1 litre/ quart of boiling water and the salt. Cover with a lid and bring to the boil, then simmer over a medium heat for 60 minutes, topping up with more boiling water as needed.)

When the lal chori dhal is cooked, release the steam from the pressure cooker slowly (or remove the pan from the heat). Drain in a sieve/strainer and reserve 125 ml/1/2 cup of the cooking water. Set both aside.

For the masala sauce, put the vegetable oil into a saucepan over a medium heat and add the cloves, cardamom pods and cinnamon stick. Sizzle in the hot oil for 20 seconds to release their aromas. Add the cumin seeds and mustard seeds and allow them to sizzle in the hot oil for 20 seconds. Add the chopped onion and salt and fry for 6–7 minutes until soft and lightly browned. Add the garlic and ginger purées, mix well and fry for 2 minutes. Add the ground turmeric, cumin, coriander and Kashmiri chilli/chili powder and mix well to coat the onion in the spices. Add the chopped tomatoes and palm sugar/jaggery, then turn the heat down to low and cook for 10 minutes until they have completely softened and melted down to form a thick sauce base.

To the masala sauce, add the cooked lal chori dhal, 235 ml/1 cup of the reserved chori dhal cooking water and the coconut milk. Stir well and simmer gently for 10 minutes.

Add the garam masala and chopped coriander/cilantro, mix well and simmer for 1 minute. By now the roasted beetroot/ beet should be cooked through and soft. Gently tip in the roasted beetroot/beet chunks (along with any residue juices), stir well and simmer together for 1 final minute.

Serve the dhal in bowls. Being quite a wholesome, hearty dish on its own, this doesn't need a heavy accompaniment, it's best enjoyed on its own or with roti breads for mopping up the sauce, if you like.

CLASSIC LAL CHORI DHAL

Grown throughout the holy Himalayan region, chori dhal, also known as aduki beans, are great in many different stews, soups and curries. This classic dish is beautifully simple and wholesome.

LAL CHORI DHAL BASE

200 g/7 oz. lal chori dhal, picked and rinsed, then soaked in 1 litre/quart lukewarm water overnight
1.25 litres/quarts boiling water
1 tsp fine sea salt

MASALA SAUCE

3 tbsp vegetable oil
1 clove
2 cardamom pods
1 tsp cumin seeds
1 tsp mustard seeds
1 onion, finely chopped
½ tsp fine sea salt
1 tsp Holy Trinity Paste (see page 13)
½ tsp ground turmeric
½ tsp ground cumin
½ tsp ground coriander
½ tsp Kashmiri chilli/chili powder
3 tomatoes, chopped
1 tsp palm sugar/jaggery
1 tsp garam masala
5–7 fresh coriander/cilantro stems, roughly chopped
Roti Breads (see page 89), to serve

pressure cooker (optional)

SERVES 4

Drain the soaked lal chori dhal, discarding the soaking water and transfer to a pressure cooker with the boiling water and the salt. Close the pressure cooker and place over a medium heat. Cook for about 25 minutes or 6 whistles. (If you don't have a pressure cooker, you can cook the chori dhal in a large saucepan with 1.5 litres/quarts of boiling water and the salt. Cover with a lid and bring to the boil, then simmer over a medium heat for 60 minutes, topping up the pan with more boiling water as needed.)

When the dhal is cooked, release the steam from the pressure cooker slowly (or remove the pan from the heat). Drain and reserve 300 ml/1¼ cups of the cooking water. Set both aside.

For the masala sauce, put the vegetable oil into a large saucepan and add the clove and cardamom pods. Let them sizzle in the hot oil for 20 seconds to release their aromas. Add the cumin and mustard seeds and allow them to sizzle in the hot oil for 20 seconds. Add the chopped onion and salt and fry for 10 minutes until the onion is softened and lightly browned.

Add the holy trinity paste, mix well into the onion and fry for 2 minutes. Add the ground turmeric, cumin, coriander and Kashmiri chilli/chili powder, mix well to coat the onion in the spices and fry for 2 minutes. Add the chopped tomatoes and palm sugar/jaggery and mix well. Turn the heat down to low and fry the tomatoes for 10 minutes or until they have completely softened and melted down.

Add the cooked lal chori dhal and reserved cooking water, stir in well and simmer gently for 10 minutes.

Stir in the garam masala and chopped coriander/cilantro. Simmer for 1 final minute and serve with warm roti breads.

SAFFRON-ROASTED PUMPKIN LAL CHORI DHAL

A hearty dish perfect for serving up to family and friends on cold autumnal evenings – soft, silky lal chori dhal is steeped in a fragrantly spiced and warming, light tomato sauce. The dish is completed with sweet chunks of saffron-roasted pumpkin stirred through, the flavour and aroma of which carries throughout the sauce.

LAL CHORI DHAL BASE

200 g/7 oz. lal chori dhal, picked and rinsed then soaked in 1 litre/quart lukewarm water overnight
1.5 litres/quarts boiling water
1 tsp fine sea salt

MASALA SAUCE

3 tbsp vegetable oil
1 clove
2 cardamom pods
2.5-cm/1-inch piece of cinnamon stick
1 tsp cumin seeds
1 tsp mustard seeds
1 onion, roughly chopped
½ tsp fine sea salt
1 tsp garlic purée
1 tsp ginger purée
½ tsp ground turmeric
½ tsp ground cumin
½ tsp ground coriander
½ tsp Kashmiri chilli/chili powder
4 tomatoes, roughly chopped
1 tsp palm sugar/jaggery
1 tsp garam masala
5–7 fresh coriander/cilantro stems, roughly chopped
Naan Breads (see page 108), to serve (optional)

SAFFRON-ROASTED PUMPKIN

1 small pumpkin, peeled and chopped into 2.5-cm/1-inch chunks (roughly 500 g/3 cups)
2 tbsp vegetable oil
½ tsp fine sea salt
½ tsp freshly ground black pepper
pinch of saffron threads
100 ml/⅓ cup plus 1 tbsp boiling water

pressure cooker (optional)

SERVES 4

Start by making the roasted pumpkin. Preheat the oven to 180°C (350°F) Gas 4. Place the pumpkin chunks in a roasting pan, drizzle over the oil, sprinkle over the salt, black pepper and saffron threads and pour in the boiling water. Roast the pumpkin in the preheated oven for 40 minutes or until softened, carefully turning halfway through.

Meanwhile, drain the soaked lal chori and transfer to a pressure cooker with the boiling water and the salt. Close the pressure cooker and place over a medium heat. Cook for about 25 minutes or 6 whistles. (If you don't have a pressure cooker, you can cook the chori dhal in a large saucepan with 1.25 litres/quarts boiling water and the salt. Cover with a lid and bring to the boil, then simmer over a medium heat for 60 minutes, topping up with more boiling water as needed.)

When the lal chori dhal is cooked, release the steam from the pressure cooker slowly (or remove the pan from the heat). Drain and reserve 300 ml/1¼ cups of the cooking water. Set both aside.

For the masala sauce, put the oil into a saucepan and add the clove, cardamom pods and cinnamon stick. Sizzle in the hot oil for 20 seconds to release their aromas. Next, tip in the cumin seeds and mustard seeds and allow them to sizzle in the hot oil for 20 seconds. Add the onion and salt and fry for 10 minutes until the onion is softened and lightly browned.

Add the garlic and ginger purées, mix well and fry for 2 minutes. Add the ground turmeric, cumin, coriander and Kashmiri chilli/chili powder, mix well to coat the onion in the spices and fry for 1 minute. Add the chopped tomatoes and palm sugar/jaggery. Turn the heat down to low and fry for 10 minutes or until the tomatoes have completely softened and melted down to a reduced and thickened curry sauce base.

Add the cooked lal chori dhal and the reserved cooking water. Stir in well and simmer gently for 10 minutes.

Add in the garam masala and roughly chopped coriander/cilantro, mix well and simmer for 1 minute. By now the roasted pumpkin should be cooked through and soft. Gently tip in the roasted chunks of pumpkin, and any spiced water from the tray. Stir well to coat the pumpkin in the sauce and simmer for 1 final minute before serving.

This is substantial enough to be served on its own or with naan breads, if you like.

MIXED DHALS

All legumes have their own characteristics and properties – some retain a firm texture and shape upon cooking, while others fall apart quickly, some are silky smooth, while others can be thick and grainy. On their own, lentils, peas and beans make wonderful meals, however, when cooked as a blend, the result can be a deliciously complex taste and texture. This chapter walks you through five recipes that showcase exactly how versatile lentils can be. Their wholesome, nutritious properties mean that they make great snacks like trail mix (see page 117), and their richness lends them well to burgers (see page 112). There's something so satisfying about the way the various textures and flavours of lentils come together to create one labour of love – I think that this is most evident in the Five-lentil Soup (see page 106), which uses a blend of channa, toor, urad, moong and masoor dhals, which means five times the flavour and five times the texture.

FIVE-LENTIL SOUP WITH CHAAT MASALA KALE CHIPS AND NAAN BREADS

A lentil soup like no other! This is packed full of powerful goodness from channa, toor, masoor, moong and urad dhal, all slow-cooked together until smooth and velvety. The soup is finished off with a topping of crispy kale chips, dusted with tangy chaat masala. They add a wonderful texture to this soup and any leftovers make a great snack.

5-LENTIL DHAL BASE

50 g/1¾ oz. toor dhal
50 g/1¾ oz. masoor dhal
50 g/1¾ oz. channa dhal
50 g/1¾ oz. urad dhal
50 g/1¾ oz. moong dhal
1 litre/quart lukewarm water, for soaking
750 ml/3¼ cups boiling water
2 garlic cloves, peeled
¼ tsp ground turmeric
1 tsp fine sea salt

MASALA SAUCE

4 tbsp vegetable oil
3 cardamom pods
3 cloves
¼ tsp cumin seeds
¼ tsp asafoetida powder
15–20 fresh curry leaves
2 onions, finely chopped
1 tbsp garlic purée
1 tbsp ginger purée
1 tsp green chilli/chile purée
½ tsp Kashmiri chilli/chili powder
½ tsp ground turmeric
½ tsp ground coriander
½ tsp ground cumin
splash of boiling water (optional)
3 large tomatoes, chopped
1 tsp palm sugar/jaggery
½ tsp garam masala
small bunch of fresh coriander/cilantro, roughly chopped
fine sea salt, to taste
lime wedges, for squeezing over
Naan Breads (see page 108), to serve

CHAAT MASALA KALE

100 g/3½ oz. kale
2 tbsp vegetable oil
pinch of fine sea salt
1 tsp chaat masala

pressure cooker (optional)

SERVES 4

Pick through the lentils to remove any stones, then mix the five lentils together, place in a sieve/strainer and rinse 3–4 times under cold running water. Soak the mixture of lentils in the lukewarm water for a minimum of 5 hours or ideally overnight, then drain and discard the soaking water.

Transfer the soaked lentils to a pressure cooker and add the boiling water, garlic, turmeric and salt. Close the pressure cooker and place over a medium heat. Cook for about 12–15 minutes or 8 whistles until the lentils are soft, thickened and pulpy. (If you don't have a pressure cooker, you can cook the lentils in a large saucepan with 1.25 litres/quarts of boiling water, the garlic, turmeric and salt. Cover with a lid and bring to the boil, then simmer over a medium heat for 60 minutes, topping up with more boiling water as needed and stirring occasionally to encourage the mixture to break down.)

When the lentils are cooked, release the steam from the pressure cooker slowly (or remove the pan from the heat). Most of the water should have been absorbed during cooking, but gently crush the lentils with any small amount that remains and set aside.

Preheat the oven to 180°C (350°F) Gas 4.

For the chaat masala kale, place the kale on a baking sheet, drizzle over the vegetable oil and toss gently to coat. Sprinkle over the salt and bake in the preheated oven for 20 minutes until crisp, using tongs to toss the kale halfway through.

Remove from the oven and sprinkle over the chaat masala. Toss well and set aside in a warm place until ready to serve.

While the kale is roasting, prepare the masala sauce. Put the vegetable oil into a saucepan over a medium heat. Add the cardamom pods, cloves and cumin seeds and let them sizzle in the hot oil for 1 minute. Add the asafoetida powder and curry leaves and shake the pan gently. Add the onions and salt, and stir to coat the onions in the seasoned oil. Fry for 6–7 minutes until the onions are buttery soft and golden brown. Add the garlic, ginger and green chilli/chile purées. Stir well and fry for 2 minutes. Add the Kashmiri chilli/chili powder, turmeric, coriander and cumin. Mix in well; if the pan gets too dry, add the splash of boiling water.

Add the chopped tomatoes and palm sugar/jaggery, turn the heat down to low and fry for 10 minutes until the tomatoes have melted and softened, stirring occasionally. Pour in the cooked lentils and stir well. Simmer together for a further 5 minutes.

Sprinkle in the garam masala and chopped coriander/cilantro and stir well.

Ladle the dhal into serving bowls and top with the chaat masala kale chips. Serve with lime wedges for squeezing over and freshly-made naan breads for dipping.

NAAN BREADS

200 ml/¾ cup lukewarm water
1½ tsp dried yeast powder
2 tsp caster/granulated sugar
350 g/2⅓ cups plain/all-purpose flour, plus extra for dusting
½ tsp salt
25 g/¼ cup chopped pistachios
1 tbsp desiccated/dried shredded coconut
3 tbsp ghee
120 g/½ cup natural/plain yogurt (at room temperature)
melted ghee, for brushing

MAKES 5

In a measuring jug/pitcher, whisk the warm water, yeast and sugar together. Cover the jug/pitcher with clingfilm/plastic wrap and let the mixture rest at room temperature for 10 minutes.

In a large mixing bowl, add the flour, salt, pistachio nuts and coconut and mix well.

Mix the ghee and yogurt into the yeast mixture and whisk gently until there are no lumps.

Make a well in the centre of the flour mixture and gradually add in the liquid yeast mixture. Using your hands, bring the mixture together to form a sticky dough. Cover the mixing bowl with clingfilm/plastic wrap and put in a warm place for 30 minutes.

Preheat the oven to 230°C (450°F) Gas 8 with a baking sheet inside.

Oil your hands and divide the mixture into 5 equal balls. Roll the balls in the palms of your hands and dip into a little flour to give a light dusting. Roll out the naan breads into circles, roughly 15 cm/12 inches in diameter and 5 mm/½ inch thick. Fold the naan breads in half, then half again to quarter-circles.

Dust with flour and, using the palm of your hand, gently push the dough into slipper shapes.

Transfer the naan breads in batches to the preheated baking sheet in the preheated oven and bake for 5–6 minutes.

Brush with a little ghee and serve.

KICHDI WITH LEMON PICKLE

Similar to the classic kedgeree, which actually evolved from kichdi, this is a recipe steeped in thousands of years of ayurvedic practices and learnings. It's a soul-hugging, comforting one-pot recipe that is said to treat illnesses while also boosting the immune system. Aside from this, it's a nostalgic dish that, for me, evokes many delicious childhood memories.

RICE AND LENTIL BASE

50 g/1¾ oz. split green moong dhal, picked and rinsed then soaked 1 litre/quart lukewarm water for 1 hour
50 g/1¾ oz. toor dhal, picked and rinsed, then soaked in 1 litre/quart lukewarm water for 3 hours
50 g/1¾ oz. masoor dhal, picked and rinsed, then soaked in 1 litre/quart lukewarm water for 3 hours
150 g/5½ oz. basmati rice
1 tsp fine sea salt
1 tsp ground turmeric
1 litre/quart boiling water

LEMON PICKLE

500 g/1 lb. 2 oz. lemons
4 tsp rock salt
1 tsp ground turmeric
2 tsp Kashmiri chilli/chili powder
1 tsp ground coriander
1 tsp ground cumin
1 tsp ground ginger
3 tbsp vegetable oil
5-cm/2-inch piece of cinnamon stick
1 tsp cumin seeds
1 tsp fennel seeds
500 g/2½ cups palm sugar/jaggery

SPICED GHEE

2 tbsp ghee
2 cloves
2 cardamom pods
1 cinnamon stick
1 star anise
1 tsp cumin seeds
2 garlic cloves, thinly sliced
2 tbsp peeled and grated fresh ginger
1 green chilli/chile thinly sliced

sterilized glass jar with an airtight lid

SERVES 5

First, make the lemon pickle. Boil the whole lemons in a saucepan of water for 8–10 minutes or until soft, then drain. Cut each lemon into eight wedges, then transfer to a mixing bowl with any juices. Sprinkle over the salt, turmeric, Kashmiri chilli/chili powder, coriander, cumin and ginger. Mix well and set aside.

Put the oil into a heavy-based pan over medium heat, add the cinnamon stick and cumin seeds and allow them to sizzle and crackle. Add the fennel seeds and toss in the hot oil for 20 seconds. Pour this over the lemons and mix well. Set aside.

Add the palm sugar/jaggery and 3 tablespoons of water to a separate pan and mix well. Set over a low heat and allow the sugar to melt slowly. Once the sugar has all melted into a syrup, add the marinated lemon wedges along with the seasoned oil and any excess juices. Mix well and simmer gently for 2 minutes. Do not let the mixture boil as the pickle will become bitter. Leave to cool, then serve or transfer to the sterilized glass jar and seal. It should last for up to 3 months at room temperature – but once opened, it will keep in the refrigerator for up to 2 weeks.

For the kichdi rice and lentil base, drain all the soaked lentils separately, discarding the water, and set aside until required.

For the spiced ghee, put the ghee into a saucepan over a medium heat until melted. Add the cloves, cardamom pods, cinnamon stick and star anise. Let the spices sizzle in the hot ghee for 20 seconds to release their aromas. Add the cumin seeds and allow to sizzle in the hot oil for 20 seconds. Add the sliced garlic, grated ginger and green chilli/chile and gently toss to mix with the ghee.

Carefully tip in the drained moong dhal and stir well into the spiced ghee. Turn the heat down to low and gently fry for 2 minutes. Add the drained toor dhal, mix well and fry for another 2 minutes. Add the drained masoor dhal, mix well and fry for a further 2 minutes.

Add the rice, salt and turmeric and mix well. Fry the rice and lentil base for 2 minutes. Pour in the boiling water, and simmer for 2–3 minutes over a medium heat. When it starts to almost come to the boil, reduce the heat, cover the pan with a lid and allow the kichdi to simmer over a very low heat for 15 minutes.

Remove the covered pan from the heat and set aside to rest for 5 minutes. Don't be tempted to remove the lid as the residual steam will fluff up the rice and lentils.

Serve in bowls accompanied by plenty of lemon pickle.

LENTIL BURGERS WITH VINDALOO RELISH AND MASALA POTATO WEDGES

Gnarly, proud and full of attitude, this gutsy dish pays homage to the iconic Mumbai street food classic, 'Pau Bhaji', but with a western twist. The traditional spiced vegetable mix is formed into a patty, with chickpeas and masoor dhal coming together to take centre stage in this mouth-watering vegan burger. Served in buns and accompanied with caramelized red onions, fiery vindaloo relish and masala roasted potato wedges, to me, this is the king of vegan burgers!

PATTIES

2 Maris Piper or Yukon Gold potatoes, peeled and chopped into small chunks
400 g/14 oz. can cooked white chickpeas, drained
250 g/9 oz. chestnut mushrooms
2 garlic cloves, peeled
50 g/1¾ oz. masoor dhal, picked and rinsed, then soaked in 100 ml/⅓ cup plus 1 tbsp boiling water for 30 minutes, then drained
40 g/1 cup vegan panko breadcrumbs
3 tbsp vegetable oil
½ tsp cumin seeds
½ tsp dried chilli flakes/hot red pepper flakes
¼ tsp ground turmeric
¼ tsp groud cumin
¼ tsp ground coriander
¼ tsp chaat masala
fine sea salt and freshly ground black pepper
plain/all-purpose flour, for dredging the burgers
vegetable oil, for frying

TO SERVE

sliced Little Gem/Bibb lettuce
sliced beef tomato
sliced red onion
6 vegan burger buns, sliced in half
Vindaloo Burger Relish (see page 114)
Masala Potato Wedges (see page 114)

baking sheet, lined with baking parchment

SERVES 6

For the patties, cook the peeled and chopped potatoes in a large saucepan of boiling water for 12–15 minutes until soft and mashable.

While the potatoes are boiling, place the chickpeas in a food processor and pulse until they are coarsely chopped. Remove from the food processor and set aside. Place the mushrooms and garlic in the food processor and pulse until coarsely chopped. Remove from the food processor and set aside.

Drain the potatoes and mash them well until no lumps remain. In a mixing bowl, combine the mashed potatoes with the chopped mushrooms and garlic, the chopped chickpeas, soaked and drained lentils, panko breadcrumbs, vegetable oil, cumin seeds, dried chilli flakes/hot red pepper flakes, turmeric, ground cumin, coriander and chaat masala. Season generously with salt and pepper and mix to evenly combine all the ingredients together.

Use your hands to scoop out 6 equal portions of the mixture (about 150 g/5¼ oz. each), and mould them into patty shapes. Make sure that you refer to the size of your burger buns so they that fit when you come to build your burgers. Space the patties out evenly on a tray and chill in the refrigerator for around 15 minutes.

Preheat the oven to 180°C (350°F) Gas 4.

Spread some plain/all-purpose flour out on a plate and dredge the chilled patties in the flour, turning them to coat all over.

Put the oil into a frying pan/skillet and, when hot, add the burger patties (depending on the size of your pan, you may have to do this in batches). Fry on each side for about 2 minutes until golden brown. As they are frying, gently spoon over some of the hot cooking oil to seal the sides of the patties.

Transfer the fried patties to the prepared baking sheet and bake in the preheated oven for 12–15 minutes to cook all the way through.

To build your burgers, place some Little Gem/Bibb lettuce, sliced tomato and onion on the bottom half of each burger bun, followed by a cooked patty. Top with a good dollop of the vindaloo relish. Sandwich on the bun lids and serve with the masala potato wedges on the side.

VINDALOO BURGER RELISH

2 tbsp vegetable oil
1 tsp mustard seeds
1 red onion, finely chopped
½ tsp salt
1 tbsp tandoori paste
2 large fleshy tomatoes, finely chopped
2 tbsp cider vinegar
3 tbsp palm sugar/jaggery
medium bunch of fresh coriander/cilantro, chopped
fine sea salt and freshly ground black pepper

SERVES 4

Put the oil into a medium saucepan over a medium heat. Add the mustard seeds and let them sizzle in the hot oil for 1 minute until they pop. Add the red onion and salt and fry for 5 minutes until soft.

Next, stir in the tandoori paste and fry for 2 minutes. Mix in the chopped tomatoes and fry for a further 5–6 minutes to allow the tomatoes to soften and melt.

Add the cider vinegar and palm sugar/jaggery and simmer the mixture for 2–3 minutes, stirring occasionally.

Season the relish to taste with salt and pepper, then add the chopped coriander/cilantro. Mix in well, then remove the pan from the heat and set aside until you are ready to serve.

Leftover will keep for up to 3 days in the fridge.

MASALA POTATO WEDGES

1 kg/2¼ lbs. potatoes (Maris Piper or Yukon Gold), cut into wedges

SPICE MIX
5 tbsp vegetable oil
1 tsp cumin seeds
1 tsp mustard seeds
1 tsp coriander seeds
5 garlic cloves, unpeeled
½ tsp dried chilli flakes/ hot red pepper flakes
1 tsp coarse sea salt

SERVES 6

Preheat the oven to 180°C (350°F) Gas 4.

Cook the potatoes in a saucepan of boiling salted water for 5 minutes or until just soft. Drain and leave in a colander to steam dry. Shake the colander around to allow the potatoes to fluff up and become slightly rough and rustic around the edges (this will make the wedges more crispy).

Add all of the ingredients for the spice mix to a roasting pan and place in the preheated oven for 5 minutes to allow all of the spices to infuse into the oil.

Remove the pan from the oven and add the potato wedges, being careful not to splash any hot oil. Coat the wedges in the oil, then put the pan back into the oven and roast for 30–40 minutes until golden brown all over. Toss the wedges occasionally to ensure even cooking.

Serve as an accompaniment.

CHANNA DHAL BHEL PURI

This dish may seem like a random mish-mash of ingredients, but that's because it's a random mish-mash of ingredients that works! A hugely popular snack originating from the bustling beaches of Mumbai – it's a combination of crispy but light puffed rice, fried or roasted channa dhal, moorish fried chickpea/gram flour noodles, glistening ruby jewels of pomegranate, crunchy fried peanuts, crisp red onion, juicy tomatoes and fresh coriander/cilantro, all bound together with a spicy green chilli/chile chutney and a tangy tamarind chutney. Once combined, the flavours all come together and sing in harmony.

3 tbsp vegetable oil
3 tbsp skin-on peanuts
100 g/3½ oz. mamra (puffed rice)
50 g/1¾ oz. fried or roasted channa dhal (also known as bengal gram)
3 tbsp sev (deep-fried chickpea/gram flour noodles)
1 tomato, core and seeds removed, finely chopped
1 red onion, finely chopped
6 tbsp pomegranate seeds
5–7 fresh coriander/cilantro stems, roughly chopped
1 tbsp green chilli/chile chutney
1 tbsp tamarind chutney

SERVES 5 AS A SNACK

Put the oil into a frying pan/skillet over a medium heat. Add the peanuts and fry in the hot oil for 1 minute, gently shaking the pan. Using a slotted spoon, remove the peanuts and place in a heatproof bowl to cool while you prepare the rest of the dish.

Combine the rest of the ingredients in a mixing bowl and stir well so that all of the ingredients are coated in the chutneys.

Stir in the cooled peanuts and serve straight away. (Because the mixture has chutney in, the bhel puri can lose its crisp texture so this doesn't keep well.)

SPICED LENTIL TRAIL MIX

100 g/3½ oz. red split lentils, picked and rinsed then soaked in 500 ml/2 cups lukewarm water for 2 hours
100 g/3½ oz. yellow split mung lentils, picked and rinsed, then soaked in 500 ml/2 cups lukewarm water for 2 hours
3 tbsp mustard seed oil
2 tbsp runny honey
¼ tsp ground turmeric
¼ tsp Kashmiri chilli/ chili powder
1 tsp sea salt flakes
10–15 fresh curry leaves
70 g/½ cup pumpkin seeds/pepitas
70 g/½ cup sesame seeds
70 g/½ cup sunflower seeds
120 g/1 cup cashews

MAKES ABOUT 500 G/ 18 OZ.

Snacking on this delightful trail mix is literally like following a trail... you don't know where the combination of flavours and textures is leading you, but you just can't stop! As highly addictive as it may be, it's also a fairly healthy snack, so feel free to indulge!

Preheat the oven to 170°C (340°F) Gas 3.

Drain both the soaked red split lentils and the yellow split mung lentils in a sieve/strainer.

Combine both types of lentils in a roasting pan and spread out well. Drizzle with the mustard seed oil and honey and sprinkle with the ground turmeric, Kashmiri chilli/chili powder, sea salt flakes and fresh curry leaves.

Toss the mixture well so that the lentils are all coated evenly. Roast in the preheated oven for 20 minutes, tossing the mixture occasionally, until the lentils are firm and crisp.

Add the pumpkin seeds/pepitas, sesame seeds, sunflower seeds and cashews and mix with the lentil mixture. Roast for a final 10 minutes, shaking the pan a few times during cooking.

This trail mix makes a great treat to snack on throughout the day, but it's also great as a soup topper, too. Store in an airtight container at room temperature and it will keep for up to 1 week.

DESSERTS

'Lentil desserts' I hear you all exclaim? Yes, that is correct! Here are four delicious desserts all made with legumes. In my opinion, this is the most exciting chapter in the book, as it proves just how versatile legumes can be – whether acting as the main body of a sweet treat or used to create a delicious filling. As they are high in protein and fibre, legumes can create highly nutritious desserts. And when they are used as flour replacements, these desserts are naturally gluten free, too. Especially in dishes like the innovative Dosa Batter Cinnamon Waffles (see page 125), where rice and channa dhal are ground together to create a waffle batter, or my favourite, the Moong Dhal Kheer (see page 120), where rice has been replaced with moong dhal to create a rich and comforting 'rice' pudding. As all good meals are rounded off with a satisfying dessert, let this grand finale of a chapter take you on a final adventure of exploring dhal.

MOONG DHAL KHEER

Kheer, also known as rice pudding, dates back thousands of years in Indian cuisine, and has links to ancient stories such as the epic Mahabharata tale. It's a widely loved and versatile dessert, which doesn't actually need to be made with a rice base. In the south of India, moong dhal is extremely popular and so is traditionally used for this dessert. Here, the natural sweetness of the dhal is accentuated with rich demerara/turbinado sugar, floral cardamom, cloves and cinnamon, and finished off with a sprinkle of flaked/slivered almonds.

200 g/7 oz. yellow split moong dhal, picked and rinsed, then soaked in 1 litre/quart lukewarm water overnight
750 ml/3¼ cups whole milk
70 g/⅓ cup demerara/turbinado sugar
3 cardamom pods
3 cloves
1 cinnamon stick
235 ml/1 cup coconut milk
3 tbsp flaked/slivered almonds, to serve

SERVES 5-6

Drain and rinse the soaked moong dhal (discarding the soaking water) and transfer to a heavy-based saucepan.

Pour in the milk, stir together and then simmer over a low heat for 25 minutes, stirring constantly. Scrape any congealed milk from the sides of the pan into the mixture as you stir.

After 25 minutes, the moong dhal should be soft. Add the demerara/turbinado sugar, cardamom pods, cloves and cinnamon stick and stir well. Simmer gently for a further 10 minutes, stirring occasionally, until the mixture has reduced by two-thirds.

Add the coconut milk and simmer for a final 5–6 minutes, still stirring occasionally.

Serve the moong dhal kheer with a sprinkling of the flaked/slivered almonds on each portion.

CHANNA DHAL HALWA

The humble halwa has ancient origins and is loved across the world. It is, in fact, an Arabic innovation, which has made its mark across the whole of India and Pakistan, as well as North Africa, the Mediterranean and Turkey, where it is more commonly known as Turkish delight. At first, you may think that using a lentil or pulse as the base of a dessert is a little peculiar, but, the chickpea has a wonderfully nutty taste, and a creamy and floury texture that is perfect to withstand the rich sweetness of halwa.

100 g/3½ oz. channa dhal, picked and rinsed, then soaked in 500 ml/2 cups plus 2 tbsp lukewarm water overnight
250 ml/1 cup plus 1 tbsp whole milk
3 tbsp ghee
70 g/⅓ cup plus 1 tsp demerara/turbinado sugar
½ tsp ground cardamom
2 tbsp chopped pistachios
2 tbsp raisins
ice cream, to serve (optional)

SERVES 2-3

Drain and rinse the soaked channa dhal (discarding the soaking water) and transfer to a heavy-based saucepan. Pour in the milk and simmer over a low heat for 45 minutes. Stir regularly and scrape any congealed milk from the sides of the pan into the mixture as it cooks.

After 45 minutes, the milk should nearly all be absorbed by the channa dhal, with only about 1–2 tablespoons of milk left in the pan. Use a stick blender or a food processor to blend the softened dhal and remaining milk to a paste.

Add the ghee to another saucepan and place over a low heat until melted. Add the blended channa dhal mixture and sauté for 5 minutes, stirring and scraping the sides of the pan with a spatula continuously. The mixture will thicken as it cooks, and it should resemble the texture of choux pastry after 5 minutes.

Add the sugar and cardamom and continue to scrape and stir, allowing the sugar to melt into the mixture, for 3 minutes.

Add the chopped pistachios and raisins and mix in well. Remove from the heat and serve the halwa warm. It is great when accompanied by ice cream!

THAI COCONUT AND RED BEAN PANCAKES

Many desserts from Southeast Asia are centred around a sweetened red bean paste. In this recipe, the bean paste makes a great rich and indulgent filling for these light pancakes, which have wonderful richness from the coconut milk and texture from the dried coconut.

PANCAKE BATTER

125 ml/½ cup coconut milk

200 g/1½ cups plain/all-purpose flour

2 eggs

1 tbsp desiccated/dried shredded coconut

½ tsp baking powder

4 tbsp vegetable oil, for frying

RED BEAN FILLING

100 g/3½ oz. lal chori dhal, picked and rinsed, then soaked in 500 ml/2 cups plus 2 tbsp lukewarm water overnight

1.5 litres/quarts boiling water

100 g/3½ oz. palm sugar/jaggery

pressure cooker (optional)

SERVES 4

For the filling, drain the soaked lal chori dhal and transfer to a pressure cooker with the boiling water. Close the pressure cooker and place over a medium heat. Cook for about 40 minutes or 14 whistles, until the beans are mushy and falling apart. (If you don't have a pressure cooker, you can cook the dhal in a large saucepan with 1.5 litres/quarts of boiling water. Cover with a lid and bring to the boil, then simmer over a medium heat for 60–70 minutes, topping up the water as needed.)

Once the dhal has cooked through, release the steam slowly or remove the pan from the heat. Drain away the majority of the excess water and transfer the lal chori dhal to a saucepan.

Place the saucepan over a low heat and mix in the palm sugar/jaggery. Cook for 10 minutes until the palm sugar/jaggery has completely melted into the bean paste, stirring occasionally. Remove from the heat and set aside until required.

To make the pancakes, combine all the ingredients for the batter (apart from the oil) in a mixing bowl and whisk until smooth. Put the oil into a non-stick frying pan/skillet over a medium heat. Spoon in enough batter to thinly coat the base of the pan, tilting the pan so that it spreads evenly. Fry the pancake for 2–3 minutes on each side until golden brown. Remove to a plate and keep warm. Repeat with the remaining batter.

To assemble, spoon a little of the red bean paste into the centre of each pancake and roll up. Enjoy warm.

DOSA BATTER CINNAMON WAFFLES WITH DATE SYRUP

Here, I've re-purposed the ancient, almighty dosa batter in the form of waffles. Soft, fluffy and as light as a cloud, these are truly a product of years of innovation. They're served with a drizzle of reduced date and cinnamon syrup, which finishes the dish off beautifully.

DOSA WAFFLE BATTER

150 g/5½ oz. dried split channa dhal, picked and rinsed, then soaked in 500 ml/ 2 cups plus 2 tbsp lukewarm water overnight

150 g/5½ oz. basmati rice, soaked in 500 ml/ 2 cups plus 2 tbsp cold water overnight

1 tbsp palm sugar/jaggery

½ tsp ground cinnamon

½ tsp baking powder

DATE SYRUP

225 g/8 oz. soft pitted dates

1 tsp palm sugar/jaggery

200 ml/generous ¾ cup boiling water

waffle machine

SERVES 4 (MAKES 8 SMALL WAFFLES)

For the dosa batter, drain the channa dhal and basmati rice separately, retaining the soaking water from each separately, too.

Using a wet grinder if you have one (or a food processor), blitz the soaked channa dhal to a smooth purée, adding up to 10 spoonfuls of the soaking water gradually to help process it down. Set aside and then do the same with the soaked rice. It's better to grind them separately because the textures of the two grains can vary. Do not yet discard either of the remaining soaking waters.

Once blended, you should be left with around 270 g/9½ oz. of ground rice purée and 460 g/1 lb. of ground channa dhal purée. Combine both mixtures in a bowl and pour in 150 ml/⅔ cup of the remaining soaking water, from the rice or channa dhal. Add the palm sugar/jaggery, cinnamon and baking powder and whisk together to form a batter similar in consistency to pancake batter. Set aside.

Combine the pitted dates, palm sugar/jaggery and boiling water in a saucepan and simmer over a medium heat for 5–6 minutes, or until the dates are very soft. Use the wet grinder or food processor to blitz the dates with the excess liquid to form a date syrup. Set aside.

To make the waffles, preheat the waffle machine following the manufacturer's instructions. Ladle in enough batter to cover the plate on one side (I use two small ladlefuls). Close the machine and cook for 12–15 minutes (cooking instructions do vary so check the instructions for your machine), then remove. Repeat for the remaining mixture; it should make eight small waffles. Serve the warm waffles drizzled with the date syrup.

INDEX

ACKNOWLEDGMENTS

Dedicated to my 'dhaling' parents and to my siblings, Bhav and Sagar, without whom this book would not have been possible. Thank you not only for being the best support network, but also for stepping in to be my hard-working kitchen assistants. We ate dhal for months on end but we made it happen! Your constant love, support and encouragement kept me from losing my sanity throughout the process of writing this book.

Thank you to Sonya Nathoo, Clare Winfield, Maud Eden and Tony Hutchinson for producing the most visually stunning photographs of my recipes. Thank you to my Commissioning Editor, Alice, for all your hard work and attention to detail. You have been incredible!

To my friends, family and foodie followers across the world who always go above and beyond to give me continuous support, strength and empowerment, thank you so much.